Praise for *Grace Lost a* ‖‖‖ ‖‖ ‖‖‖‖‖‖‖‖‖‖‖ ‖‖‖ ‖‖‖
D0195182

"Once I started reading *Grace Lost and Found,* I could not put it down. I was struck by how deeply Mary Cook wove the process of spiritual recovery into her work. A must read for those seeking wellness."

    —Pia Mellody, Senior Clinical Advisor for The Meadows and author of *Facing Codependence*

"Mary Cook's *Grace Lost and Found* is filled with helpful information about not only recovery from addictions, but the complexities of life in general. From feeling helpless to realizing personal choices and responsibility, each section brings the reader to thought-provoking questions and affirmations to understand growth through adversity. Individuals and professionals alike could benefit from this book."

    —Barb Rogers, author of *If I Die Before I Wake* and *Twelve Steps That Can Save Your Life*

"Articulate, compassionate, and non-judgmental, Mary Cook writes with a clarity and warmth that makes the reader want to keep reading. It is one of those books that readers will want to pick up more than once, knowing that every page will offer them guidance and support in their journey."

    —Barbara Joy, author of *Easy Does It, Mom*

"In the fine book *Grace Lost and Found* Mary Cook gently invites readers to share her journey of hope through the angst of addiction. A very worthy book for those who suffer and for those who know people who suffer. I strongly recommend it."

—Karen Casey, Ph.D., author of *Codependence and the Power of Detachment*

"Mary Cook's *Grace Lost and Found* creates the opportunity for a deeper understanding of addictive behavior and recovery. It provides more than information . . . it provides a process for personal reflection."

—Stephanie S. Covington, Ph.D., author of *A Woman's Way through the Twelve Steps*

"Mary Cook helps people find the treasure in their problem. I prefer not to have people become strong at the broken places, but help them to learn from their pain, so they're better able to bend and become strong enough to not break. *Grace Lost and Found* is an empowering resource for abandoning and healing the wounds of your past, surviving, and thriving in the face of adversity and rejection, and creating your authentic self."

—Bernie Siegel, M.D., author of *365 Prescriptions for the Soul* and *Faith, Hope & Healing*

Mary Cook's *Grace Lost and Found* contains a wealth of information. Here is the place to find answers about all those thorny 'what is this about' questions people have when confronting addictions and mental illness. The book overflows with compassion and insight."

—Earnie Larsen, author of *Stage II Recovery* and *The Healer's Way*

Grace Lost *and* Found

Grace Lost
and Found

from addictions *and* compulsions

to satisfaction *and* serenity

MARY COOK, M.A., R.A.S.

Conari Press

First published in 2010 by
Red Wheel/Weiser, LLC
With offices at:
500 Third Street, Suite 230
San Francisco, CA 94107
www.redwheelweiser.com

ISBN: 978-1-57324-468-8
Library of Congress Cataloging-in-Publication Data is available upon request

Cover Designer: Kathryn Sky-Peck
Text Designer: Donna Linden
Production Editor: Michele Kimble
Copy Editor: Laurel Warren Trufant, Ph.D.
Proofreader: Nancy Reinhardt
Typeset in Goudy Old Style and Perpetua
Cover photograph © BLOOMimage/Getty Images
Author photograph © Jim Lund

Printed in Canada
TCP
10 9 8 7 6 5 4 3 2 1

The paper used in this publication meets the minimum requirements of the
American National Standard for Information Sciences—Permanence of Paper
for Printed Library Materials Z39.48-1992 (R1997).

To Jeffrey

*I smiled at you and you spoke of fear that chased you like a
monster in the dark.*

*Your attempts to flee on artificial highs reinforced your pain
and gave you more to dread.*

*So young and needing love and comfort, when trauma took
you from your home.*

*Pain and darkness stole your life force, deprived you of your
heart's desires.*

*Reprieve finally came, but you found it impossible to make up
for immeasurable loss.*

*The scar couldn't cover your terror, that you were broken and
would never be filled.*

*Reaching outside yourself became an obsession. Gratification
fueled the need for more.*

*Tortured now by continual craving, you mistook your shadow
for your self.*

*Until one day, you courageously surrendered the artificial life
for what was real.*

*You learned to follow direction from those who'd gone before
you.*

A new way of life with steps and traditions, a fellowship based
  on principles and purpose.
Service to others gave honor and value, and led you to recall
  the wholeness of your soul.
It was after this time that I finally met you. I saw a man
  haunted by past despair.
And I saw an amazing dancing soul, with stars in his eyes
  and dreams on his mind.
Your tears and tenderness gave you the strength to stay for
  once, where you were safe.
Your wisdom and willingness gave you grace, your humor
  broke through the clouds.
I saw your highest truth and you saw mine. God was
  everywhere, inside of me and you.
Guiding two souls fulfilling a mission. And all we knew was it
  could not be otherwise.
You helped me to see the depth of giving and receiving,
and the power of prayer and healing.
I lost you from this earth, but not from my heart.
You kept on giving from the Heavenly realms.
I believed before, but you led me to knowing,
that souls are eternal and we never stop growing.
This book is dedicated to you, Jeffrey Dillwood.
Childhood trauma, pain, and addiction could not extinguish
  the highest truth;
that God is always in us and the greatest power is love.
Thank you Jeffrey, for opening my heart so profoundly to
  God's love.
Thank you for continuing to help me,
in extending light and love from your celestial home.
  Love always, Mary

Grace Lost and Found

Table of Contents

Chapter 4

The Process of Growth and Transformation   132

Acknowledgments

I AM LOVINGLY GRATEFUL TO MY HUSBAND, Jim Lund, for his unwavering strong encouragement, support, and assistance in all areas of my personal and professional life. He is a consistent advocate for my happiness, health, and fulfillment. I am thankful also, for his psychological and spiritual understanding and for his creativity, talents, and wisdom in his own parallel life journey.

I am grateful to my family, friends, clients, students, conference attendees, and readers for their encouragement to write this book, and their own examples of transforming negative patterns into positive growth.

I extend thanks to all of the members of the Beacon House Association of San Pedro in California. The Beacon House is a men's social-model residential program for addiction that is unparalleled in terms of the depth and breadth of treatment and strong, long-term support. My friend, Bill Maddox, the Program Director, uses the text of Alcoholics Anonymous, his potent observation, keen insight, and guidance from God to provide treatment to countless men. His concern for the physical, mental, emotional, and spiritual well-being of each individual is inspirational. I also thank Luis Lozano, the Executive Director, for his talents and ability to keep the Beacon House thriving at a time when addiction treatment for those without finances or insurance is scarce. I also appreciate his role in the outstanding reputation that Beacon House maintains in all of the surrounding communities.

I thank all of the staff at *Steps For Recovery* for publishing my monthly articles since 2001, most of which appear in this book. *Steps For Recovery* is a professional newspaper that does an exemplary job of keeping the recovery community well informed.

And last but not least, I am grateful to authors, books, bookstores, libraries, and publishers for providing perpetual pleasure, inspiration, and enlightenment to my ever-inquiring mind.

Preface

I INVITE YOU TO JOURNEY DEEPER into healing and wholeness. Learn the psychodynamics of your symptoms and compulsions. Discover treasures buried beneath your pain. Identify and relinquish negative energies that sabotage healthy success. Find the needy, wounded child within, and positively transform this aspect of yourself. Cultivate relationships based on spiritual principles. Live with surprise, awe, and wonder. Understand and embrace body, mind, heart, and spirit. Experience the healing power of God's grace.

This collection of essays is for people who have addictions, compulsions, negative thinking, or other unhealthy responses to living. It is also for their significant others, and for professionals whose clients exhibit these problems. The book is for all members of the great variety of 12-step programs, of which Alcoholics Anonymous was the first. I believe that anyone interested in psychological and spiritual insight and improvement will benefit from reading this book.

Each essay is followed by personal growth questions and affirmations. They are intended to give practical insight and motivate you to take specific positive actions. My ideas are a blend of psychodynamic theory, spirituality, and 12-step-program philosophy. You may read the book as subjects call to you, highlighting favorite sentences or paragraphs. You can use the affirmations to exchange false beliefs for solutions. When you add positive emotion and visualization to affirming statements, they become more effective. Alternatively, if you are doing this work with a counselor, sponsor, or support group, it may be best to go through the essays in the order presented. It is wise to allow someone to hold us accountable, and to support and reinforce our personal growth commitments.

I also highly recommend that you journal your responses to the essays, your answers to questions, and any positive changes you experience. Prioritize your personal development goals from answering the questions. Write down active measurable solutions and practice them on a daily basis. Once a new positive behavior feels more comfortable and consistent, select another solution to practice.

A daily ritual of reading, journaling, affirmations, prayer, and meditation is most beneficial, especially in the morning. Begin with ten or fifteen minutes, and expand over a period of time. Continual healthy growth is our true nature, not just remission of symptoms. All negative experiences are meant to move you into healing, character development, increased compassion, understanding, service to others, surrender of defenses and defects, and deeper communion with your Higher Power.

This book is not intended to replace visits to the doctor, counseling, treatment, or 12-step-program participation, but rather to deepen and enrich what is already helping you. The words "steps" and "program" in the text refer to the twelve steps and to all 12-step programs. Feel free to substitute your own words for "Higher Power" or "God" if your beliefs are different from mine. I believe there are many names and paths to the kingdom of the Almighty. I further believe that the highest form of love is what we find there. May you be blessed in your journey.

Introduction

Snapshots from My Life

I WAS BORN IN TUJUNGA, CALIFORNIA to a father, mother, and a dog named Debbie who also thought she was my mother. We lived in a small, rustic home that had been converted from a chicken coop. We were surrounded by trees, birds, mountains, and sunshine. My smile took up half my face. Thus began my lifelong love of nature and animals. I was very close to my maternal grandfather, who came from Minnesota to visit his first grandchild and promptly decided that he too wanted to live in a place where it was green and flowers bloomed year round. He was a gentle, humble man who modeled what I now know as spiritual principles. He knew God was with him in every breath, and he lived in unconditional gratitude.

My family moved frequently, traveling throughout the U.S., Europe, and eventually Australasia. I always wrote, first in my imagination and later on paper. I was an extremely shy child, preferring animals, books, natural environments, and personal reflection over my peers. I felt surrounded by Heavenly spirits and never felt lonely. Traveling expanded my view of life. I had great adventures in castles, museums, forests, tropical islands, and the endless red sand and rocks of Central Australia. Indigenous peoples living in ancient traditions fascinated me.

At night I had a different life. I had nightmares of being chased, captured, and tortured in every imaginable manner. I walked and talked in my sleep, thrashed around and threw things, seemingly fighting demons. I sometimes woke up rolled up like a mummy in the covers at the bottom of the bed. Even in the daytime, I loved finding hiding places and fantasized the perfect adult life alone in a simple hut in the woods.

I was a teenager in the 1960s. Debbie and my grandfather were both dead. We were going to live in the same home for several years—something we had never done before. I worried that I would have to make friends. I was angry, confused, and sad. I tried alcohol, other drugs, recreational sex, fasting, meditation, and relationships, and none of it felt right. I wrote pessimistic poetry and sang songs of despair. I wanted to understand myself as well as I understood the characters in stories. But I was in the middle of a mystery.

Through an administrative "error," I was enrolled in a high school modern dance class. I choreographed dances by listening to music, until I saw the entire dance as a movie in my mind. Despite my shyness, I didn't mind performing, because I was absorbed in the creative experience. Dance gave me greater sensitivity to emotion, body language, and physical communication, and helped me with my adolescent angst. I continued dancing for several years. I now know that this performing prepared me for future speaking in front of hundreds of people.

In early adulthood, I fell in love with psychology. I taught myself to speed-read through books, lingering at the parts that felt the deepest and richest to me. I analyzed my dreams and fantasies, and began to feel that I was standing on more solid ground. A college professor suggested that I obtain a job in counseling, and sent me to interview at a substance-abuse treatment center. I was hired and told to attend 12-step meetings so that I could understand this integral part of treatment. I loved the honesty and openness in the meetings, the generosity and humility in the fellowship, and the wisdom and thoroughness of the steps. I learned about the universality of human feelings, no matter what the outward behaviors.

A couple of years later, I attended a private graduate school. The school mandated that part of our training be spent in our own individual and group psychotherapy so that we could directly experience the process rather than just read about it and discuss it. I am grateful for this gift, and for how it propelled me to spend many more years in therapy, gaining an increasingly deeper understanding of myself and life. This blend of academic and experiential work allowed me to see clients clearly, without the distortion of projection, transference, judgment, or unrealistic expectations.

Following graduate school, I was asked to teach at a university in their Alcohol/Drug Counseling Certificate Program. My work with alcoholics and other drug addicts taught me to dive into the core of the problem, decipher the psychodynamics of destructiveness, and quickly arrive at behavioral, cognitive, emotional, and spiritual solutions. This was a life-and-death matter. Much later, when my practice expanded to people who had no addictive history, my clients expressed surprise and gratitude that I could pinpoint their problems and possibilities so easily.

But I also knew that it wasn't up to me to save people. It was their choice to live in the problem or take steps toward solution. My task was to enlarge their view and understanding of themselves, their options, and the consequences of their choices. The longer I counseled clients, taught, wrote, and meditated, the more metaphors and meaning, messages, and healing I experienced. Clients, students, and people reading my articles responded positively to my work, and increasingly urged me to write a book.

One day, I was asked to help a man who had advanced hepatitis C. I immediately sensed a strong bond between Jeffrey and myself. I helped him heal childhood trauma and was privileged to spend a great deal of time with him—and to be at his side when he died several months later. I felt a strong presence of God whenever

I was with Jeffrey. He reignited my spiritual growth, helping me to focus on soul energies, spiritual healing, and soul purpose. He has been of enormous assistance to me and my work since his transition to Heaven. My conscious contact with God and Heavenly spirits from my childhood returned and rose to a new level. I understand the value of darkness in life as an opportunity to delve into deeper truths and higher consciousness. I see problems and pain signaling us to surrender all that holds us back from our highest good. I see loss as reminding us that our greatest gifts are within, and that true love is eternal.

I believe that fear is the root of negativity. The desire to reject what we don't want and capture what we do want is the beginning of a false self and a false life. My response to childhood was to keep my life small and simple so I could control it. But when we attempt to escape or to over-control our lives, we deny what needs healing and our wounds increase. I was afraid of people and inner demons. I suffered over the loss of those few I trusted. I didn't know what to do with anger and confusion. I acted out negatively as a result. Suffering, symptoms, stress, and despair tell us that we're going in the wrong direction, and attempt to motivate us to reexamine ourselves.

Today, I want my life to be as large as God wills it. As I face my fears with curiosity and compassion, they become helpful guides. I can be grateful for the time that I have with loved ones, knowing that everyone is on loan from Heaven. When I surrender what doesn't work and meet the mystery of the Universe with as much positive energy as I can, it moves me forward.

I believe that how we're wounded can lead us to our soul's purpose. I believe that willfulness directs us to the heart of our darkness. I believe that we're meant to wander far from Heavenly grace, so that we're certain of our commitment upon returning. I believe that there are no limitations on blessings and miracles. I heartily welcome and thank you for joining me on this journey back to grace.

Chapter 1

Addictions, Compulsions, and Recovery

EVEN IF WE WERE BORN GENETICALLY predisposed to addiction and were chronically given drugs and traumatized in our childhood, we are still responsible for our adult lives today and for our recovery. Acting out, hostile dependency, rebellion, and vindictiveness serve only to keep us bound to an unhealthy past and to people who harmed us. Typically, we direct aggression toward those whom we see as responsible for our harm, toward ourselves, and toward anyone who at least unconsciously reminds us of our pain and conflicts, including our children.

Wherever our negative feelings or actions are aimed, recovery urges us to redirect this energy toward resolution. Maintaining negativity toward ourselves deepens

our wounds. Maintaining negativity toward others reinforces attachments to problematic behaviors and attitudes. Needing or wanting others to change so that
we can heal keeps us stuck in unfulfilled childhood dependency. All of these scenarios recreate familiar pain
and problems and we feel increasingly less capable and
confident in our lives.

The Solution Is Up to Us

Not one of the twelve steps tells us to seek amends from
others. Recovery relies only on our changing to more
mature behavior. Inherent in addiction is avoidance of
appropriate responsibility. We court illusions of power
through picking up weapons, rather than weeping for
lost innocence and protection. We hide pain through
altering perceptions of internal and external reality,
rendering us helpless to find solutions. We create false
selves from defensive adaptations to dysfunction, and
then wonder why we feel so alone and empty. Our relationships reflect impoverishment and degradation. We
are dishonest, disloyal, diseased, and devoid of true love
and wisdom. We sit on a massive mountain of wreckage
waiting for a short dose of counterfeit paradise from a
bottle, needle, or pipe. We are in no position to hold
others accountable at this stage. We must desperately
desire recovery with the same passion with which we
pursued drugs.

The 12 steps are designed to help us recognize our unhealthy patterns and from whom and from what experiences they originate. Exploring our early lives in the fourth step yields the most valuable information in this regard. We may learn that our destructiveness to ourselves or others is a response to unhealed abuse or trauma in childhood. Perhaps we married someone who seems cold, critical, and distant like our fathers were. Codependency and controlling behaviors may stem from being over-responsible for an addict parent. Deprivation of important psychological needs may have resulted in compulsive stealing. Childhood sexual molestation can trigger later prostitution. Unhealthy family enmeshment may translate into fear of relationships. Whatever problems we suffered in childhood, they were not due to our being impossibly challenging children, nor because we deserved the treatment we received. It is our responsibility, however, to transform dysfunction into new healthy thinking, feeling, and behavior.

Dysfunction comes from the giving and receiving of unhealed wounds by imperfect people. Recovery comes from creating a loving and understanding relationship with ourselves, which is modeled on our perception of how God relates to us. The aim of examining early problems is to correct our response to them today. We encourage ourselves to own the full depth and range of feelings that were triggered by the harm we recall. We respond with attention, compassion, comfort, and containment. Containment means feelings can be experienced, expressed, and explored without acting out, condemning, judging, or losing control. Emotional healing emerges from repeated sharing of painful experiences with the accompanying feelings, until anger, anxiety, and fear are greatly diminished.

We examine how childhood problems influenced our thinking in order to identify and begin detaching from false beliefs that perpetuate negativity. Our minds absorb everything in childhood, and these experiences and our reactions to them create the first and most powerful framework from which we understand life. We need to change our identities and life beliefs so that they no longer reflect defensive reactions to pain and problems, but rather incorporate spirituality and recovery tools for healing and growth. We can practice a more positive relationship with ourselves by treating ourselves with affection, consideration, respect, and sensitivity. When confronting ourselves, we focus on learning and solutions, rather than harsh judging. We incorporate discipline and structure that promotes the achievement of healthy goals. We detach from people, places, and experiences that are toxic to us, and set boundaries and limits that help us maintain recovery as our first priority. Through daily prayer and meditation, we seek God's guidance and support toward spiritual wellness. Whatever we have suffered, our solution lies in appreciating the gift of life by refraining from destructiveness and making positive use of our God-given talents and interests.

Personal Growth Questions

1. In what ways do I express negativity toward myself and others?
2. What part of myself and my current life reflects childhood pain and problems?
3. What must I change in myself to resolve early and current conflicts?

Affirmations

I am capable and willing to learn and demonstrate positive productive behavior.

I practice loving and understanding myself today.

Habit-Formed Thoughts and Feelings

Dominant thoughts and feelings experienced in childhood and in active addiction tend to recur even when the elements that prompted them are no longer present. If, for example, I was abused as a child and my dominant feeling was fear, I will experience fear despite the safety of my current adult environment. If I was abandoned in childhood, felt a deep sense of loss, and believed that I was unlovable, these will be my issues in adulthood. If stimulant drug use brought feelings of intense nervous energy, which I directed to excessive activity, I will continue to experience this in sobriety. If my dominant feelings when withdrawing from stimulants were depression, despair, and lethargy, then I will also have these feelings in sobriety.

When we experience feelings and thoughts that are out of sync with current situations, we tend to create circumstances that justify them. So we focus on who or what we can't trust to explain our fears. In relationships, we magnify behaviors that we view as signs of withdrawal, which reinforces our belief that we are not loved sufficiently. We obsess on what needs to be done and compulsively busy ourselves in frenetic activity when we have nervous energy. We dwell on our shameful pasts and overwhelm ourselves with impossible visions of what we must do in order to recover. And this drains our energy and explains our feelings of hopelessness.

Making decisions and acting from habitual patterns ensures that our lives remain predictably sick. And risking the least amount of change in recovery increases vulnerability to relapse. Our thoughts and feelings have more power to affect our behavior than external circumstances. Thus it's vital that we pay attention to them and consciously decide which ones to empower, which ones to explore, and which ones to relinquish. When our thoughts and feelings harm more than they help, when they intrude more than they support, or abuse and control more than they teach and guide, we are not free to create the lives we so deeply desire and deserve.

Our minds present a chaotic mass of mixed messages, all fighting for control over our decisions and actions. The disease disguises itself to talk to us in a multitude of ways, as do our character defects until we surrender them. Aggression, arrogance, defensiveness, drama, fear, judgment, prejudice, pride, and shame typically have strong voices in our heads. Just as in experiencing cravings to use drugs we must interrupt our thinking long enough to view the ultimate consequence, we must do the same when listening to other sick messages in our minds. Aggression spreads woundedness like wildfire. Arrogance halts learning and growth. Defenses prevent us from healing and invite further attack. Drama substitutes a hell of a soap opera for a life. Fear removes faith. Judgment binds us to whatever we judge. Prejudice and pride turn our character defects into dictators. Shame supports inferiority and punishment rather than amended behavior and relationships.

We can't afford to empower our minds in recovery. This is one reason why fellowship, following direction, sponsorship, step work, prayer, and meditation are stressed in the program. Clarity, peace, and wisdom will come as we cleanse ourselves of old mental patterns. Relaxation and meditation techniques are the most important tools to interrupt our normal mental process. As thoughts fade away, we tune in to a deeper part of ourselves. Here, there is nothing to control, no effort to expend, and no conditions on caring. Full absorption in the present moment allows us to detach from all that pulls us away from our spiritual origins. In the light of serenity, our habitual thoughts and feelings seem infantile. Yet we see with the eyes of compassion, not judgment. We allow ourselves to surrender, on a daily basis, that which we have outgrown.

When we cease listening to our minds' chatter, stop seeking fulfillment outside of ourselves, and surrender defenses and offenses, we discover that everything in our lives is here to teach us. We then see that our strength lies in love and service. When we give up our small wills that cling to crumbs of comfort, in exchange for our Higher Power's will which provides eternal abundance, we are given our greatest gift. The enormity of change that is required for quality recovery cannot be achieved through human power alone. It is our consistent conscious contact with our Higher Power that allows us to trade habit-formed thoughts and feelings for a greater truth that sets us free.

....

Personal Growth Questions
1. What are my negative habitual thoughts and feelings from the past?
2. What conflicts occur as a result of them?
3. What positive thoughts and feelings could replace them?

Affirmations
I consciously choose healthy role models today.

I practice quieting my mind and feeling the peaceful presence of my Higher Power.

....

Grace Lost and Found

Commendable Communication

Most 12-step programs advise us to speak from personal experience and feelings as opposed to opinions, philosophy, and generalities. We are told to tell our truth and let others tell theirs. "Live and let live" allows us to respect autonomy and accept differences. Thus, we do not force our beliefs onto others or assume that everything stated in a meeting applies to us.

We are educated about self-talk and learn to distinguish between the addict and the recovery parts of our dialogue. We learn effective intervention techniques that increasingly disempower our old sick thinking. We also practice compassionate confrontation and supportive statements to strengthen our recoveries. The more we are consciously aware of our internal dialogues, the quicker we are to identify and prevent or halt disguised relapse behaviors.

The formula to share "experience, strength, and hope" and the focus on helping newcomers enables us to identify and develop recovery tools. It shifts our thinking of ourselves as having either nothing or only bad inside, to seeing how we have something good enough to pass on to others. As we help others, we reinforce our own recoveries. We are told that the program works on attraction, not promotion, so we know we must be good examples.

Writing gratitude lists and not giving up before the miracle arrives helps us to develop a broader, more hopeful, positive attitude. The disease wants us to think, talk, and act negatively, and to believe that drugs alone will save us from this misery. Expressing thanks to others allows us to experience bonding with trust and reciprocity. Appreciating what we do have and valuing character strengths further increases the distance between us and the disease.

If our focus was taking from others in our disease, then it's important to practice appropriate giving in recovery. Instead of statements aimed at manipulating another, we let others know what we appreciate in them. We practice active listening and make commitments to be of service. If we were used and abused in our disease, we need to learn healthy boundaries and state what we will and will not accept today. In this case, we ask ourselves if helping another would either enable them or distract us from our own responsibilities and recovery needs. If that is the case, we practice saying "no."

We are asked to identify and take responsibility for our part in conflicts with others. We are told to use our recovery principles rather than focus on whether others are doing so. We are encouraged to state our feelings when someone upsets, angers, or hurts us, and to take responsibility for our healthy solution, since we are powerless over others. In contrast, when we focus on others' character defects and how we want them to change, they become our solution and we become victims. This dependency causes more anger, pain, frustration, and depression.

We also learn that communication is not just the content of words. The process part of communication includes attitude, body language, feeling, inflection, timing, and tone. These things significantly alter the meaning and credibility of the words. When there's disparity between the words and the process, the process is what is received and valued. We can easily disguise or deny our reality with words. It's considerably more difficult to do so with the elements of the process. Paying conscious attention to this intrinsic part of communication gives us additional tools for deeper personal and interpersonal awareness.

Completing a fourth and fifth step gives us valuable information for identifying triggers to emotional pain. We are hypersensitive and hyper-responsive to experiences and interactions that remind us of unhealed past wounds. An overly strong reaction to a current situation indicates a need to explore earlier conflicts and their consequences. When we work through feelings regarding early-life traumas, we can appreciate the differences between the current and previous experiences. The unmanageable crisis of today becomes manageable when we realize we are not helpless, dependent children, but adults with solutions and resources as large as the fellowship and as powerful as the program's spiritual principles.

Taking responsibility for our recovery from trauma means that we identify and work to change false beliefs internalized from those who harmed us. It also means that we change behaviors that resulted from our adaptive responses to unhealthy situations. Our healing does not require assistance from those who mistreated us. It does require us to identify communication to ourselves and others that originates from trauma. This is similar to differentiating the addict and recovery parts of our minds. When we hear statements reflecting what we learned from a sick environment, we intervene with affirmative, solution-oriented dialogue.

Our beliefs form the basis for our behavior and determine how we talk to ourselves and others. Recovery allows us the opportunity to transform sickness into health in every area of life. Practicing commendable communication is an important piece of this journey.

....

Personal Growth Questions

1. What is the importance of autonomy for myself and others?
2. What are the differences between the sick parts and the healthy parts of my inner dialogue?
3. What are specific examples of how recovery changes my communication?

Affirmations

I communicate honestly and respectfully and take healthy responsibility for myself today.

I am a person of integrity because my words match my feelings, beliefs, and actions.

....

What's the Inside Got to Do
with the Outside?

Externalizing is a defense that is overused in addictions and compulsions. It means that, when we feel something painful internally, we look for an outside fix or focus. Sex, drugs, food, shopping, and gambling are common examples of fixes. They offer the temporary illusion of love, protection, pleasure, power, and excitement, and they dull or numb the conscious awareness of pain and stress. Additionally, when we are uncomfortable with self-examination and with acknowledging our own feelings, we frequently create external conditions that mirror our internal battles.

We may be very angry with ourselves and initiate arguments with others. This allows us to focus on other people rather than on our own conflicts. We may feel chaotic, disorganized, and messy inwardly, and attract people and situations into our lives that reflect the same confusion. This lets us deny or minimize our own inner states and imagine that our problems are external. We can obsess over someone else's messiness. When we struggle between our will and our higher purpose, or between supporting or sabotaging ourselves, this conflict can manifest in external people and situations. We then focus on the outside disagreement as the source of our confusion. If we have a fear of airplanes and, on our next flight, we sit next to someone with a greater fear of flying, we may well find ourselves comforting and reassuring this person. If we're having a day full of pain and depression and we reach out to help others, our own discomfort seems to diminish or disappear entirely.

As with any defense mechanism, there is a proper time and place for externalization. Often, when addicts enter treatment, their focus is not on finding solutions for their active addiction (the internal problem), but rather on maintaining a license, regaining custody of children, avoiding incarceration, divorce, homelessness, etc. Our actions, feelings, and thoughts play a primary role in determining the outcome of these experiences. Yet we commonly believe that the symptoms and consequences of these things are the source of our problems. When defenses are used temporarily, and/or when we have no awareness of more direct tools, they may well serve our best interests at the time. If, however, we use defenses for problem resolution beyond the point of necessity, or following the acquisition of additional abilities and maturity, then we need to evaluate their possible misuse. The hope for addicts who begin recovery with external motivation and focus, for example, is that they ultimately redirect their focus to the core problems inside.

We change actions first in recovery, because feelings and thoughts take longer to transform. This is the correct beginning, because negative behaviors concretize negative thoughts and feelings. Abstinence from negative actions thus fails to make them real. This eventually gives us the opportunity to see them for what they really are— attempts to repeat familiar scenarios to try and protect ourselves from potential harm. They originate from a time when we had no other tools or insight to cope with stress other than defending or offending behaviors.

Just observing negative thoughts without holding onto them or pushing them away causes their energy to dissipate. Calm, nonjudgmental reflection also affords us an opportunity to better understand our thoughts and feelings and their transient nature. Finally, this technique demonstrates that we are much greater than any thoughts or feelings. We do not need to fear or empower them to determine what we do or say. When we take appropriate action despite whatever internal or external circumstances arise, we no longer need to maintain the energy and tension from past negative experiences, nor do we attract more negativity by imagining similar episodes. This then allows us to be increasingly receptive to spiritual assistance, since significant or chronic negativity interferes with our ability to commune with our Higher Power.

The greater value we place on exterior over interior life, the more we compromise courage, emotional maturity, identity development, self-esteem, stability, and understanding. Whether negative or positive, all that we focus on and have strong feelings about in our outside lives is somewhere inside of us. Recovery is a time to examine our actions, feelings, and thoughts to ascertain what supports and what imperils our highest purpose. When we give authority to reasoning above impulses, intuition above mental chatter, and faith in our Higher Power above our own will, we live in sync with our divine plan. When we accept personal responsibility for understanding ourselves and supporting our well-being and growth, we attract external conditions that mirror this serenity.

....

Personal Growth Questions

1. What is my outside focus when I feel pain or discomfort inside of me?
2. How does this outer focus affect me and my problem?
3. What are healthier responses to address my pain?

Affirmations

I am learning to live in greater harmony inside myself and in my life.

The more focused I am on the task at hand, the more overall serenity I experience.

....

A Puzzling Paradox of Purpose

We are born with divine light shining in our eyes. We are blessed, united, wide open, and whole. There is no end to our potential; we behold everything with awe. From our original home, we bring unbounded love, unbridled joy, and bountiful peace. We are here because our souls yearn to grow.

So we descend into the uncertain garden, forgetting our purpose and plan. We begin to feel fear more than peace. Instead of unity, we notice separation, jealousy, and judgment. Often, we see more pain and sorrow than joy—more abandonment, abuse, and hatred than love. Our vision darkens and we see ourselves as inferior and incomplete. We become shadows on the earth with barely a glimmer of the higher truth.

Experiencing significant pain can lead us to believe that life is a battlefield and that choice lies in the degree of energy we invest to build fortresses for protection and armaments for destruction. Energy additionally goes into finding false substitutes for peace, unity, joy, and love. Sickness, ignorance, and fear now hold tremendous power over us. This is how we invite more negative experiences into our lives. Who we are becomes the story of life's damaging blows coiling around us like a deadly python. The more we attempt to appease or fight this snake, the less we recall of our divine origin

And yet, ultimate impending doom can open us up to solutions. It is not our physical death, but the death of this paradigm of living that offers us hope. Brilliant discoveries and inventions come to those who think outside the given constructs of reality. What enables us to do this is an awareness of consciousness existing apart from our minds and personalities. When we witness ourselves in thought, feeling, or action, and begin to question the effectiveness of how we are living, we find a key. We are not merely physical minds and bodies. There is something greater than this, observing us.

We typically do not question the meaning of life or our individual purpose when we sit on the comfortable sidelines of contentment. Long leaps forward are neither contemplated nor attempted without a metaphorical fire at our heels. Autonomy and personal freedom are far more precious following a period of enslavement. Feeling the pressure and constraint of deceit can cultivate a deeper commitment to honesty and openness. Abuse and abandonment can awaken greater love and compassion.

We must think beyond our five senses, our minds, and society's norms in order for these transformations to occur. The more we are dissatisfied with life, the more changes we must make within ourselves to correct this. What is familiar, habitual, and seemingly protective drains us of our true life force.

This earthly duality presents a puzzling paradox. Since all things exist, how can we remain aware and make conscious healthy choices without taking up arms against the opposite side? How can we live in harmony with love and hate, harming and healing? The answer lies in learning to see the deeper truth and growing beyond its disguises.

All actions communicate something important. Negative actions communicate what we feel happened to us, and how we are stuck there. When we aren't able to articulate this in meaningful understandable ways to others, we are drawn to act it out. If I've been bullied, humiliated, and rejected and feel unable to communicate the pain of these experiences to others, I may treat others in these ways so that they develop a personal understanding. Or if I am afraid of others' reactions to this behavior, I may mistreat myself. In both cases, I am communicating in actions that I have been hurt, have lost trust, and remain stuck in this painful place because no one understands me and the help that I need.

Once we realize there is a deeper level of communication and understanding, we are free to make choices that do not cause harm to ourselves and others. When we believe that we are spiritual beings temporarily in physical bodies for purposes of learning and growth, we can see painful experiences as a sign that love is blocked. Walking through these experiences allows us to understand more completely the profound effect of specific deprivations and abuses. When we commit to a thorough examination of ourselves and our lives, this allows us to determine and learn to demonstrate the highest form of transformation from these painful experiences.

Mature love does not offer Pollyanna sentiment or coercive schemes. Mature love arises from deeply seeing, understanding, and valuing ourselves and others. We cannot live the answers to our questions until we have sufficiently lived and understood the problems. It is through this process of living, learning, and transforming that we discover and attain our unique purpose in this life.

Personal Growth Questions

1. What is the worst pain I have experienced? How has it affected my life?
2. How did I attempt to protect myself and/or act out aggressively as a result of this pain?
3. What is the highest spiritual transformation of this painful experience? How will I think, feel, and act when I achieve this?

Affirmations

I am willing to surrender old protections
that hamper my spiritual growth
and embrace loving solutions.

I choose to respond to conflicts in ways that
cultivate greater insight and maturity.

When Wishes Become Willfulness

When what we want is what we can provide for ourselves, life seems good. When what we want depends on circumstances beyond our control, life doesn't seem to be as good. When our wishes are tools for self-examination and ongoing development, we draw something positive to us. Pure, sustained focus on our wishes without making decisions or taking action gives us greater understanding. When the essence of our wishes is revealed, our responses are wiser. When our wishes are not explored and understood, their acquisition fails to satisfy us. When these wishes are unmet, or turn into expectations that demand fulfillment, we draw negativity to us. This is one of the ways in which we work against ourselves.

When our primary feeling is gratitude and wishes are bonuses, we're autonomous. When wishes become obsessions crowding out awareness of blessings, we're enslaved. When we give our wishes to our Higher Power to see if they're in sync with our soul's purpose, we're following spiritual principles. When we control, deceive, manipulate, or threaten in order to attain our wishes, we work against our Higher Power.

When wishes spring from our hearts, they are a sign of love. When they arise from our egos, they are a sign of fear. Perception of reality when based in ego, fear, and will results in a life emptied of meaning and true fulfillment. Perception of reality based in unity with our Higher Power and divine purpose results in a life overflowing with riches that money, power, and prestige cannot procure.

What does not come freely to us is not truly ours, and our self-worth will decrease. Coercion creates conflict, debt, and pain. This negative energy distances us further from the lives we wish to live. Conversely, what we attract as a natural outcome of our spiritual growth will reflect the inner harmony that we possess at the time, and our self-worth will increase. Affirming and sharing what is holy within us results in contentment, perpetual abundance, and happiness.

If our identities stem solely from earthly conditioning, we are in fragments going in all directions, pretending to be whole. From this perspective, fear is the dominant force and willfulness its voice. Our lives are then fraught with confusion, discontent, insecurity, and separation from what we most need. If our identities recognize their spiritual origin, we know we are united with all we ever need and all of life. In this view, love is the primary authority and wisdom its voice. Life is thus continuously creative, as creation is the offspring of love.

If we deny death, we may focus our wishes on things that externally provide the pretense of a self-centered life at peak functioning. Because this is not the center of our true selves, we feel out of balance and empty, no matter how many wishes are satisfied. If we fear death, it follows that we fear change, for every change is a little death. Our wishes may then be for that which offers the illusion of sameness, security, and stability. Since we are constantly in motion, the tension required for us to remain static is immense and will drain our natural energy. If we see death as a welcoming back to our original home, our wishes are more likely to reflect spiritual growth and giving. This also brings a greater celestial feeling to life on earth.

Willfulness comes from denial of who we truly are and inhibits our development. Dependency on external sources to satisfy wishes leads to anger, disappointment, and symptoms of ill health. Our outer lives evolve from our inner lives. Therefore, when we feel deprived of something positive, it represents a blocking of love within us. When we feel overwhelmed by something negative and wish for its departure, it indicates our need to surrender something negative within us. Wherever love is blocked and negativity is bound, we suffer. Willfulness magnifies this problem. Being mindful of our external wishes can direct us to our corresponding inner work. We must surrender the deceptive beliefs that limit true love and promote false pride. Ego-based, willful lives make us beggars. Divinely inspired lives lead to wishes that signal our soul's purpose and fulfillment.

....

Personal Growth Questions

1. What is an example of willfulness and an example of a healthy wish for me?
2. What inner work do I need to do on my willfulness?
3. What is one way I can extend spiritual love beyond what I'm currently doing?

Affirmations

*I realize internal abundance
and creative fulfillment.*

*I have a never-ending supply of love and
gratitude to share with others.*

....

How Do We Heal?

When we only treat symptoms—whether behavioral, emotional, or mental—symptoms recur. Symptoms are present to alert us to examine ourselves in order to determine what is not working effectively. Chronic lack of joy, humor, and serenity, or excessive anger, anxiety, and fear create emotional illness. Persistent blaming, seeing everything as a catastrophe, deceiving, judging, and worrying cause mental disorders. Habitual behaviors of abuse, aggression, over-controlling, and manipulation lead to conduct disorders. Abstaining from specific actions and from expressing certain feelings or thoughts helps us immensely in early recovery. When there are powerful dynamics at the root of illness, however, failure to decipher the message in the symptom means we will manifest new symptoms.

Chronic negative thinking impacts our relationships with self, with others, and with our life experiences. It diminishes motivation, effort, and full involvement in tasks, and discourages us from obtaining the assistance we need. We are then more vulnerable to fail or fall well below our potential in whatever we do. When our feelings typically lack positive energy or contain a preponderance of negative energy, our natural vigor for life is significantly diminished. We then rely on energy from anger, anxiety, or fear to fuel us. This energy does not help us learn and mature.

Anger energy is an attempt to experience power in response to a feeling of powerlessness. It is forceful and punishing. It attempts to prevent harm or retaliate in response to harm through aggression, intimidation, or threat. The false belief that reinforces aggressive energy is the idea that simply expressing thoughts, feelings, or actions originating from anger releases us from past, current, or potential future anger or harm. In truth, this response attracts more anger and harm into our lives.

Anxiety energy keeps us compulsively busy and obsessively thinking. It is a scheme to keep our bodies so busy and our minds so bogged down in details that we don't sense the larger perspective of our personal life issues. Anxiety generates a belief that we are making progress and being productive. This progress, however, is rarely in sync with our primary goals.

Fear energy primarily goes into protecting, guarding, planning counterattacks, and reinforcing outer strengths. Unless there is imminent, definable, or observable danger from something that we can avoid through our own efforts, fear energy is not productive or positive. However, we typically believe that mental or behavioral fortresses will allow us a peaceful existence within them. On the contrary, they engender greater conflict.

Overall, operating from anger, anxiety, or fear adds to the negative energy of the problem. This narrows our thinking and perspective, heightens our stress, and opposes healthy solutions. When we desire positive change and healing, we must experience the problems and our conditioned responses to them—without defensiveness, decision making, or actions. This allows us to become aware of a part of us that is detached from problems and pain. We can learn how to identify problems and responses without making them who we are. We can view them as visitors with a message, rather than as lifetime attachments or appendages.

Problems indicate that we are being given opportunities to learn and grow. Symptoms are a sign that we are not learning, but rather resisting our lessons. Pain is a call for healing. Yet for healing to occur, we must make space for it, prepare for it, and welcome it. Most of us, sadly, never do this. Instead, we fill ourselves to overflowing with anger, blame, hate, judgment, and vindictiveness, or with despair, self-pity, shame, and victimization.

Harm comes from misunderstanding. Abandonment comes from fear. What sets us free from fear and harm is understanding and faith. To be set free, then, we must engage in an ongoing process of surrender. Like answers to our prayers, what opposes the goal of our prayers is made abundantly clear to us so that we know what to surrender. When we pray for love, typically hate, jealousy, and fear of rejection show up. When we pray for peace—chaos, conflict, and crisis commonly occur. These are the answers to our prayers. We are shown exactly what prevents us from achieving our goals and, therefore, what to relinquish. When we examine within us what we wish to relinquish, we see how these responses originated, how we attached to them, and how we actively recreate them through our beliefs.

The process of understanding these problems prepares us to let them go.

Our Higher Power is greater than all problems and pain. Therefore, our connection to our Higher Power is the place where healing occurs. This is where we can view internal and external experiences as visitors to teach us higher truths. We can realize the attachments that we must surrender in order to grow. And we are comforted knowing that the most important part of us—this place of divine connection—can be forgotten and closed off from conscious awareness, but cannot be damaged, diminished, or destroyed.

....

Personal Growth Questions

1. What important lesson have I learned as a result of feeling and processing pain?
2. What are the ways that I have grown from directly addressing problems?
3. How do anger, anxiety, and fear affect me today?

Affirmations

*I open myself to wisdom and healing
whenever I experience pain.*

*I willingly surrender false beliefs
that prevent true understanding.*

....

Healing for Clients and Counselors

Whether clients or counselors, students or teachers, we are all imperfect human beings. We are here because we yearn to grow. And the strongest motivator for growth is pain. When we are significantly harmed, or deprived mentally, emotionally, or physically, and have no safe people or role models to help us understand and rebound or heal, our minds create defense mechanisms and coping strategies to hide our real pain and vulnerability. This may serve us well over a short time period, but backfires in a longer time frame. When we become habituated to our means to hide painful reality, we forget our true selves behind the fabrications.

As counselors, we can only help clients to grow as far as we've grown. If our efforts to assist are sincere, this keeps us in the forefront of ongoing personal recovery. We must see beyond our own false selves, past the wounded and the wounding parts, to our divine origin and the courage and yearning to grow therein. When we, as professionals, have genuine whole identities and positive self-esteem based on deep, thorough recovery work, then we have no difficulty surrendering our personal ego-focus when working with others. This allows us to give full presence, emotional attunement, and openness to understanding clients as unique individuals. This means that we are alert and able to halt tendencies to project our issues inappropriately or transfer the dynamics of our personal relationships onto our clients.

Additionally, we are able to identify and apply feedback to clients that also fits our current growth needs.

The depth and extent of our own work reminds us how necessary compassion and understanding are to promoting positive change. When we resist, minimize, or deny who we and others are, change is impossible. It is our focus on continued personal growth that primarily determines our helpfulness to others. Without personal growth, our years of education and experience allow us only superficial management of problems. For it is not so much what we say as counselors that effectively assists clients, but who we are as people and what feelings, thoughts, values, and integrity we exhibit as we interact with those we help.

As counselors, we must give what we feel the client is prepared to receive in order to stimulate their growth, rather than incite greater defensiveness. We give our perceptions, information, and understanding to clients. Because we have learned to see beyond our own defenses and our own false selves, we respond to the client's true self as well as what they outwardly present. We see their strengths, gifts, hidden fears, and vulnerability. We see the healthiest part of them as well as their sickness. This also helps us remain in an empathetic and growth-promoting role, rather than an adversarial or sympathetic, co-dependent one.

Counselors who absorb their clients' pain and assume responsibility for their wellness sabotage their clients' growth, create a foundation for an unhealthy hostile, dependent relationship, and are attempting to control others over whom they have no control. Clients lose even more self-esteem in this process. They ultimately resent the counselors despite the initial appeal of someone accepting their responsibilities for them. The false idea of the client being defective or incomplete and therefore needing an external "fix" is reinforced. In this situation, the counselor loses the ability to be effective with clients and cannot be effective in his or her own recovery either, because no one can heal pain and resolve problems that are not their own.

Clarity about our own identities and boundaries, and acceptance of what we can and can't change, means that we respect clients' rights to make their own decisions—and to reap the consequences, enjoy the rewards, or learn from the experience. We know that God does not revoke our free will no matter what harm we commit by abusing it. Furthermore, recovery tells us that we inspire growth in others through positive example rather than persuasion. All of this reminds us of the need to demonstrate appropriate patience and tolerance, and places the outcome of the therapeutic relationship clearly in the hands of the client and his/her own Higher Power. Our part as counselors is to facilitate a safe process where clients may heal and grow if they so desire.

As counselors, we must understand the consequences of traumatic experiences, chronic painful feelings, and negative thinking to assist clients with emotional healing. We examine the effects of these things on our clients' mental and emotional states, physical health, relationships, careers, self-esteem, spirituality, and overall outlook on life and the world. To help clients gain this insight, we must have extensive reflection in these areas of our own lives. Furthermore, we must not take personal offense to the understandable hypersensitivities of clients who have unhealed trauma. Something about our appearance, manner, professional position, or words may remind them of others in the past who were not trustworthy and harmed them. If we are able to identify and avoid imposing our own projections and transferences onto clients, we can help them to understand and eventually learn to do the same.

The ultimate goal in emotional healing is to transcend trauma, so that it no longer has any negative power in our lives. If we were sexually abused, for example, our purpose is to transform our identities as sex or sexless objects to whole, healthy, unique individuals, to embrace positive feelings about our bodies and their caretaking, to rediscover and love our true selves, and to realize healthy empowerment in our lives. If we were abandoned, our task is to reclaim, listen to, understand, honor, and love our true selves, to attract others who are naturally inclined to do the same, and to assert boundaries with those who have nothing to give or who would be toxic to us.

Not all of the information that helps us in personal recovery and counseling comes from our minds. Our bodies store memories, hold tension and repressed feelings, and speak to us in the language of physical sensations and symptoms. We also have associations, creativity, dreams, intuition, synchronicities, visions, and divine guidance. Again, the more we as counselors have explored and benefited from these realms of important messages for ourselves, the more we can effectively incorporate them into the counseling process.

The courage to face and transcend pain and trauma deepens our ability to enjoy mutually rewarding relationships with ourselves and others. It is relationship dynamics that harm us, particularly in childhood. So it is critical that we, as counselors, work deeply to heal ourselves. Active recovery means that we remain honest, humble, open, and teachable. The dynamics between counselors and clients can either facilitate healing and growth, or reinforce confusion and negativity. No matter who we are, what our history has been, and what we currently do, our purpose in life is to use all of our experiences as opportunities for learning, healing, and growing.

....

Personal Growth Questions

1. How do I hide painful reality? What are the characteristics of my false self?
2. In what area of my life do I have the most integrity? Discuss how my actions, beliefs, feelings, and statements are congruent in this area.
3. What are my co-dependent tendencies and failures to respect my own or others boundaries?

I am willing to examine myself deeply
and heal anything that interferes
with my health or happiness.

I embrace honesty, humility, respect,
sensitivity, and integrity in my relationships.

....

Grace Lost and Found

We are born of divine grace and promise. Life on earth, however, rarely supports this. We feel flawed in response to mistreatment. We think we are not whole when our needs and wants are not met. We accept the model of life we hear about and see from others. We define who we are from how significant others wish us to be. We lose awareness of our unique greatness when our environment does not reflect this. We lose intrinsic value and purpose when our energies are needed for basic psychological and physical survival.

All the while, we feel a yearning for something far greater than our personal experience. We search for it in our surroundings and find what is readily available. We try people, hobbies, food, drugs, sex, or gambling. We receive temporary satisfaction and believe that, if we can only procure an endless supply, it will be sufficient. Somehow, the more we receive, the more we need and the more deficient, lost, and broken we feel. The inability to contain and understand this painful dynamic often breeds violence. Whether verbal or physical, this fails to satisfy as well. So we may try not feeling at all. And again, we experience only temporary relief. At this point, death may be attractive, if we believe that only it will relieve us of our pain.

We may, in this crisis, reach beyond what is familiar and enter treatment. If we didn't feel at rock bottom before treatment, treatment will eventually bring us to this state. For us to heal and grow, we must admit all that works against our health and happiness. People, places, and things that formerly allowed us to feign security and esteem are exposed, for all illusions prevent growth.

We see how sickness arises from feelings buried alive. We see how destructive attacks on ourselves and others proceed from denial. We see how our attempts to reduce conflict and obtain our own version of safety and security result in escalated threats and danger. We see how tiny our lives are as a consequence of chronically contracting from pain. We see that controlling our lives causes us to lose awe and wonder, how imposing dominion over others costs us our freedom within. We see that petty reactivity and dressed-up defensiveness betrays our true nature. We now understand that we were never flawed, deficient, inferior, lost, broken, or alone. These were our responses to hurtful and traumatic actions and attitudes. They are not meant to define us and dictate our lives.

Recovery affords us a new model of life and a new way of being. Our minds fight it, for it is unfamiliar. We are afraid, for it requires a conscious choice to be vulnerable. We must surrender all defenses and walk back through the pain inside of us and in our lives. We can only choose our highest path when we've heard and understood all parts of ourselves. We are here to listen, not just with our ears, but with our hearts fully open. We are here to act, not from our mental patterns and habits alone, but from intuition and messages received through prayer and meditation. We are here to understand and evolve, not solely by following the given earthly framework, but by seeking our soul's purpose in life experiences. We discover that there was nothing wrong with our yearning for something far greater than our personal experiences. The problem was that we could not see it with our eyes, because it is not material, but ethereal. It is the magnitude of our Higher Power's love for us. We rediscover it deep inside us, upon clearing away false beliefs and misguided actions.

We don't have to buy friendship or sex. We don't have to cheat, lie, or deny. We don't have to put anything we cherish, including ourselves, in harm's way. We know that right actions and thinking lead us to friendship and love. We know the whole truth is the only thing that frees us from bondage. We know the difference between a healthy risk for spiritual growth and a plan for sabotage. We deserve to walk the path of spiritual greatness and let go of all that hampers our way. Our minds are like infants that accept and adapt to life on earth. Our souls are elders that know we are here to transform earthly experiences into grace and promise, of our own free will and effort.

....

Personal Growth Questions
1. What have I searched for thinking it would numb my pain or make me whole?
2. What were the results of this search and how did I feel afterward?
3. What can I stop defending and face? What can I stop pretending and accept?

Affirmations
I am complete and I am loved.

When I look deeply, I see that my life is filled with wonder and grace.

....

Soul Guidance

When we seem blocked from spiritual progress, we are likely listening to the wrong source of inner guidance. We are both human and spiritual. Our minds dictate advice based on the culture and habits of our families, society, and environment, while higher consciousness offers our souls perspective.

Our human minds give us what we need to function in our specific social system. We learn to master tasks, acquire abilities, and define and meet goals that give us a sense of esteem and empowerment. Our five senses help us determine our particular responses to stimuli. We seek gratification of desires and needs, and avoid pain and confusion. We, in the Western world especially, experience materialism, which emphasizes security and power through abundant finances, competition, and consumerism.

We are here with a deep longing to learn, experience, and evolve, according to our character traits and talents, and their potential. We and our lives are dual in nature; they blend healthy and unhealthy, knowledge and ignorance, attraction and repulsion, stewardship and exploitation, wealth and impoverishment. Earthly life is not meant to be perfect bliss and harmony. The key to accomplishing our purpose, however is to attend equally to both human and spiritual aspects and discern between the two.

When we are significantly harmed or deprived in early life and have no resources to heal, our minds' focus can become dominantly fear-based. This, then, propels a preponderance of defense mechanisms to protect our physical or psychological survival. Fear and its reactions make it difficult for us to appreciate the balance of what our minds can give us. The excess of fear can cause us to fixate outwardly, both to blame and to seek relief in order to avoid internal examination. Since we cannot control others and outside experiences, however, we only accumulate more fear through this method. Fear also disrupts our ability to hear from our souls. We often realize the flaw in this chronic over-focus at a much later time.

The voice of fear is loud, repetitive, insistent, and frequently illogical and insane. We are threatened, called names, and given disaster scenarios of what will occur if we fail to heed fear's advice. Fear is an intrusive bully that attempts to control and smother us with its self-appointed power. And yet, it is the culmination of this long, painful, overwhelming experience that can motivate us to an earnest search for spiritual truth and blessings. We tend to take for granted that which is always with us and revere more strongly that of which we have been desperately deprived.

And how will we know the voices of our souls? One way is by their stark contrast to fear. Our souls' voices remain silent if we do not wish to hear them, for they need nothing from us and are not bound by time or space. When they speak, they will not give us more than we can understand and wisely use. Soul enters our conscious awareness where we have created space and cultivated gratitude for its offerings. Soul guidance is gentle, soft-spoken, and devoid of all judgment. It is accepting, calm, encouraging, unconditionally loving, patient, and understanding.

Our souls will not help us cause harm or rob anyone of free will. They will not codependently rescue us from problems we must experience in order to learn and spiritually evolve. Soul sees through false disguises, defense mechanisms, and character defects to show us that it is our own shadows that scare us the most. These shadows need only the light of love and truth to be transformed.

Whenever we feel blocked from spiritual growth, we can ask what actions, feelings, or thoughts hold us hostage. We can imagine, and then practice demonstrating, their surrender to our Higher Power. We allow ourselves to align with the divine increasingly, while at the same time accepting the imperfection of our humanness. In this way, we experience healthy, unconditional love and commitment to ongoing progress. As we continue to ask and listen for soul guidance, fortresses of fear fall down around us to reveal the blessings that have always been with us.

....

Personal Growth Questions

1. What percentage of my average daily focus is on human concerns and what percentage is on spiritual matters? How do I feel about this?
2. What dominant actions, feelings, and thoughts represent my most important human and spiritual concerns?
3. What are my reactions and solutions to fear that are not precipitated by realistic, imminent danger?

Affirmations

I create time and space for soul guidance and I express appreciation by following the direction given.

I equally accept my human and spiritual responsibilities for learning, growth, and helpful service to others.

....

A New Model for Maturity

In our childhood, dependent state, our safety, security, and happiness are irrevocably tied to our immediate social environment. When this environment lacks the capacity to provide necessary physical and psychological functions for our well-being, we become wounded.

The areas of self or life that are not negatively impacted in childhood are free to evolve. We mature through a process of trial, error, exposure to new information, and training and modeling through a variety of people and experiences in our lives. The wounded areas, however, generally remain in an immature state. In absence of healing, defenses arise to protect us partially from full awareness of present and future pain. These defenses eliminate or reduce opportunities for growth. As our social environments change and expand through life, our responses in these obstructed areas remain static, until we develop the courage and desire to examine and change ourselves.

The deepest and most enduring wounds usually occur in childhood. Because a clear whole sense of identity has not yet formed, we see our child-selves primarily as reactors and responders to others who have power over us. Since thinking in these wounded areas remains static, we continue to over-empower others as the source of our safety, security, and happiness into adulthood. This means that, in every part of our selves and lives that hold unhealed wounds, we lack the personal awareness and responsibility necessary to experience mature health and happiness. Furthermore, we believe the problem lies either in others or in our lack of skill to change others so that they can take responsibility for our well-being.

Thus we search for significant others to compensate and correct for previous painful experiences. If we were abandoned as children, for example, this can translate into seeking a relationship with someone who never does or says anything we could perceive as a potential rejection. They don't interact or speak with anyone that triggers our jealousy, insecurity, or sense of inferiority. They cannot become angry with us or hurt us; they cannot withdraw affection or warmth without us feeling abandoned. If we were abused as children, we may look for partners who are always kind, compassionate, sensitive, loving, and understanding. They must not raise their voices, become angry, critical, confrontational, controlling, impatient, intolerant, or argumentative, even for short periods of time, without us feeling endangered.

These examples hopefully illustrate the impossibility of the "right partner" being the solution. To further complicate matters, as human beings, we are easily habituated to patterns of acting and thinking, and to attracting people who reflect our unresolved issues. Our patterns eventually become automatic and unconscious, to the point that we believe our current experiences confirm the past, even when no objective observer would validate this.

We erroneously think that we need someone to gratify our needs today in such a magnified and perfect

way that it eradicates the feeling of our past deprivation forevermore. This is unrealistic. When we focus
on what we missed and need, we reinforce and attract
more experiences of missing and needing, rather than
experiencing gratification. The nature of habituation
also means that we become attached to our specific
problems and pain, and their resulting symptoms and
defenses, and are reluctant to give them up. We perceive them as an important part of our identities and
even our survival strength.

This accounts for us not believing, internalizing,
and reinforcing positive experiences that can be a part
of the healing process. When we do obtain gratification
for what we seek, we tend to dilute it with defenses,
rather than accept it with gratitude. Because we are
looking for a complete healing to come from others,
we reject and resist anything short of this. We focus on
how the gratification hasn't lasted long enough yet, or
likely isn't sincere. Or we set new, higher requirements
for gratification.

Healing and maturity don't come from others. They
come from inside of us with the help of others. They come
from allowing defensiveness to decrease, internalizing
positive experiences, giving positive energy to ourselves
and others, and processing and releasing past negativity.
Experiencing all of our feelings without clinging to them
or fighting with them allows them to evolve.

The heart of our life journey is contained in the
closed-off places within us. Hidden behind every wound

is a great gift waiting to be discovered. If we think of the highest possible outcome of problems and tragedy, we get a glimpse of the power of spirituality and our soul's purpose.

Our world is filled with examples of the worst possible outcomes. Abuse breeds more abuse, more victims and perpetrators, more alienation, distrust, fear, and violence. Abandonment leads to depression, emptiness, enmeshment, manipulation, and worthlessness. Committing to recovery means we take the road of our highest purpose and set new models for maturity and fulfillment in all areas of our lives.

....

Personal Growth Questions
1. What did I need in childhood that I did not receive?
2. What did I receive in childhood that was harmful to me?
3. How do these issues in childhood impact me and my life today?

Affirmations
I choose to practice giving to myself and protecting myself in healthy ways.

I am understanding and outgrowing all false beliefs and defenses.

....

A Way of Seeing

When I need what is not mine to receive, my ego is
in charge. When I include myself in the wonders of
creation, I am not separate from what I need. When I
fight against my own pain, I add toxins to the wound.
When I compassionately feel the pain, the wound is
cleansed and dressed. A baby crying can elicit our love
or resentment, depending on how we feel toward the
infant inside of us. Parched earth can lead us to water
the land or embitter us to the lack of sustenance. It
depends on how much the darkness of deprivation has
obscured the light of hope for us. Someone in a rage
can trigger our own anger, escalating the damage. Or
it can remind us of how much suffering there is in the
world and reinforce our refusal to participate in it. It
depends on whether we see the world as victims and
aggressors, or whether we see violence as a symptom
of ignorance and uncontained pain. Arrogance and
self-righteousness can incite debate and divisiveness,
unless we understand it as fear pretending to be pride.
To understand another, we must look deeply within
ourselves. To understand ourselves, we must see beyond what our minds think we are.

   We begin our lives depending on others for survival, thinking that they are a part of us. We communicate in cries and coos, smiles and screams. Some needs
are met and we feel whole and hopeful. Some needs are
not met and we may even be punished for having them.
Then we feel fragmented and threatened. Our opinion

of ourselves is formed from how important others treat us. The amount of fear we experience determines the quality of our survival and sets a pattern for how we see the world. Without tools to address painful feelings and unmet needs, we defend against them. This creates more internal and external conflict. Defensive responses give the original problem more power and tend to instill fear and create problems for others as well.

We wonder why we feel chronically angry, depressed, and empty. We are flawed and our lives are incomplete because that is the nature of the human condition. Yet our mission is much larger than the human condition. When we fail, fall, or falter, we have a chance to be free of harsh judgment and unworkable expectations. When we are beaten, bleeding, and broken, we can embrace a benevolent attitude toward all suffering. Painful admissions, empty ambitions, and broken hearts invite a larger truth. Just as admitting powerlessness and unmanageability over addictions invites, not just a solution, but a whole new way of seeing and behaving, continual suffering and struggling in any area of our lives can be transformed with a spiritual perspective.

Our actions, feelings, experiences, and thoughts are not our identities. A redwood tree is not just the parts that we see. The roots and foundation allow the tree to live, just as our divine origin nourishes and sustains us. And just as a tree needs soil, sunshine, nutrients, and water, and provides cleaner air, shade, and homes for animals, we are interconnected and interdependent on each other. The more our lives honor our spiritual roots, the better examples we are for others. If we wish for greater harmony, peace, and understanding in the world, we do not look for change in anyone else. We must initiate change, through our own practice of identifying and letting go of all that is within us that hampers our highest wishes.

We are so much more than we think ourselves to be. We walk in the midst of grace and glory, yet our minds see misery. Great success does not come from a list of accomplishments. It does not come from money, possessions, or power. It comes from listening to our hearts, our instincts, and, most of all, our God. It comes from loving ourselves with all of our defects. It comes when we lay down weapons and offer assistance. We must cease defending, denying, offending, and prejudging. Compassionate caring, dignity, grace, humility, and understanding—that is what we should be extending.

In the end, all that matters is how well we have loved ourselves, others, this earth, and the Creator of it all. Our ignorance of this larger truth costs us untold suffering. It is the test of this life to meet pain with understanding, exchange fears for faith, and know that we are continually nurtured by what we cannot see. This is the greater reality.

Personal Growth Questions

1. When do I perceive myself as a victim? As an aggressor?
2. What knowledge and tools do I lack at these times?
3. What does recovery teach me about victimization and aggression?

Affirmations

*I choose not to defend or offend,
but to support my own growth and examine
life experiences compassionately.*

*I am open to a whole new way of
seeing and behaving that allows me
to reach my highest potential.*

Chapter 2

Responses to Stress, Fear, and Pain

WHEN WE DON'T KNOW HOW to address and resolve
problems and pain, we attract more of the same. When
we neglect to support and develop joy and natural talents, we forget we have them. When we fail to listen
to our instinctual wisdom, it falls silent. Not taking responsibility for our health and happiness holds us hostage to the influences of others. Basically, turning away
from our real selves and our internal processes leads to
a life based on projections of what we want and don't
want, and little to no satisfaction or fulfillment.

Everything we deny in ourselves we see in outward forms in our lives. If we deny anger, we attract
and focus on angry people. If we deny our own lack
of responsibility, we have continuous altercations with
people who are irresponsible. If we deny pain, we react

to others' pain with codependence, irritation, or avoidance. Denying our hopes and dreams makes us cynical, suspicious, and envious of those who work toward their dreams. When we can't find the good in ourselves, we think the world is withholding our treasures. If we deny love within us, we complain that nobody loves us. If we deny self-hatred, we are full of rage in our reactions toward others.

Watch What You're Projecting

Projections empower other people, places, and things well beyond what is realistic or healthy. The end result of this is that we have no idea how to meet our own needs and wants. Habitual ways of thinking and acting wear a deep groove in our minds and become the only life we know. When our thinking is primarily negative, we change positive experiences into negative ones by believing they won't last, that they can't be trusted, or that they require too much effort to maintain.

People sometimes think the key to changing negative patterns is affirmations and forced positive thinking. This only works if we are also understanding and resolving past feelings, thoughts, and behaviors that are harmful. Positive thinking that covers up denial and fear only brings more issues to deny and fear.

Compulsions are an end result of projections, whether we are running from or toward something. We don't know how to control chaotic thoughts and feelings, so we compulsively clean house or attempt to control others. We don't know how to relieve pain and experience joy, so we drug ourselves to do the job. We don't know how to comfort or nurture ourselves, so we overeat. We end up with houses that are never clean enough, people that don't do as we wish, and drugs and food that fail to satisfy and can ultimately kill us.

The solution lies in taking back our projections. We can ask ourselves what it is that we hate, fear, love, and yearn for within us. When we spend too much time obsessing over people, places, and things, we must firmly redirect our focus to our own attitudes, beliefs, feelings, and actions—both negative and positive. When we identify a problem, it's important to understand it as fully as possible and ask where we can grow and what steps to take to get there. We need a deep and honest self-appraisal, with the intent to understand, learn, and improve ourselves and our lives. We need to commit to different action that is specific and beneficial to our taking healthy responsibility for our well-being today.

....

Personal Growth Questions

1. What do I dislike in life that mirrors a problem or defect in me?
2. What is one area where I'm avoiding personal responsibility?
3. If I take responsibility for mature change in this area, how will it affect my life?

Grace Lost and Found

....

Recovery from Trauma

Picture a desperately sick heroin addict fixing in a dirty bathroom, or a crack addict barricading doors against imagined intruders. Now imagine a recovering addict for whom lovemaking with a healthy partner triggers sick and dirty feelings, or a recovering man living a healthy, productive life but imprisoned by a past identity so deserving of harm that it is imagined at every opportunity. No doubt there is greater illness in the first scenarios. However, many recovering people who are committed to their program remain haunted by past harm, especially if it occurred in childhood. They cannot fully internalize and enjoy the gifts of recovery, and their symptoms are a cry for help.

Trauma leaves deep imprints on us. It may not go away just because we practice a healthy life today and have worked our steps. As we acquire increasing support, success, resilience, and maturity, we may become aware of past trauma that was previously denied or repressed. Or we may realize a deeper level of feelings, thoughts, and/or behaviors associated with the trauma. Unhealed wounds may be triggered by elements associated with the trauma, as well as experiences that are its polar opposite.

If we were chronically beaten as children, then loud voices, confrontations, criticisms, yelling, and hitting can trigger the memories. But so can nurturing, comforting, understanding, and compassionate responses, because they remind us of what we lacked as children. They can trigger memories of desire that we had to deny to make the pain of abuse more manageable. We also internalize a negative image of ourselves as unworthy of love in response to repeated abuse or mistreatment. When others treat us badly in recovery, it can trigger our childhood feeling response. And when others treat us as worthy today, it can remind us of the pain we suffered when we were deprived of this, as well as the vulnerability we felt having these needs in a climate where they were rejected or responded to in a humiliating or hostile manner.

When children are victims of incest or abused in other ways by a parent or caretaker, they internalize the abuse as their own wrongdoing. They carry shame, disgust, horror, fear, and a deep sense that they are unlovable. They learn that they are mere objects for others' sick needs. They try to hide themselves and fear there is no protection or safety—perhaps no God. There are countless associations connected with the abuse: sights, sounds, smells, tastes, and touches directly related to the actions of the abuse and the environments in which it took place. These are all triggers for unconscious memories.

Children incorporate myriad defenses to ward off the destructiveness of this pain. Denial, dissociation, repression, idealization, identification with the aggressor, and rationalization are all common. Later, we often see behaviors like prostitution, self-mutilation, active addictions, eating disorders, psychosomatic illnesses, phobias, domestic violence, and violence toward society. When we live in a dysfunctional system, we adapt in a dysfunctional way to cope with it. These adaptations and the false beliefs we internalize about ourselves, our relationships, and our lives are then based on sick models. When these beliefs and adaptations are made in childhood, they are extremely resistant to change. They were our means to survive and cope as best we could at our most vulnerable time in life.

In order to realize that we are worthy of love and a fulfilling healthy life when we've experienced significant deprivation or abuse, we must heal the pain from all the years of its denial. This is not an easy task. Sometimes, we remain in old negative identities, attempt to fix the pain with compulsive good works, or redirect energy and attention into other excessive activities. Some of us with histories of abuse develop phobias against any kind of confrontation or criticism, thinking that, if we can ward off or refute it today, it will not re-stimulate old trauma and thus we will feel healed. This does not result in healing. Furthermore, this fear-based behavior short-circuits needed growth that comes from deeply knowing both our strengths and our weaknesses.

There is a healing process involved with all abuse, whether we suffered at the hands of others or damaged others or ourselves. This process includes recalling trauma and talking about it repeatedly in order to remember what occurred behaviorally, what feelings and thoughts were triggered, what defenses were used against the pain, how we made sense of it, how we adapted and changed ourselves to cope, and the consequential symptoms arising from trauma in our bodies, minds, emotions, spirits, relationships, and lives. When we are ready to do this work, it is crucial to find people who are safe and healthy, and who understand this process of healing in order to let go of deeply ingrained patterns. Our full enjoyment of recovery's blessings and miracles depends on this.

....

Personal Growth Questions

1. What are some of my remaining imprints from trauma?
2. What defenses did I use to cope with trauma that are in my life today in some form?
3. How do these defenses and imprints affect me now? How would I like to change in these areas?

Affirmations

I will attract safe, healthy people who will help me heal and grow.

I'll let go of toxic people and experiences and their effects, so I can see myself as I truly am.

....

Owning Our Pain

Enslavement to craving renders mature, healthy, spiritual thinking and behavior impossible. Craving comes from feeling incomplete. We are incomplete when we refuse to see parts of ourselves. We are incomplete when we imagine our pain is unique, or too small or too great to be healed. We are incomplete when we perceive a particular feeling or experience as our identities or our lives. We are incomplete when we believe that our problems and solutions are outside of us. We are incomplete when we fail to see our connection with others or with our God. All of this belies and grossly underestimates who we truly are.

Denial of our whole, real selves gives rise to false selves that focus on possessions, power, and prestige. We try to make permanent what is inherently transient and wonder why peace eludes us. All of life is in continual flux. To attempt to make constant what we think gives us joy is a blind, massive exercise in futility. We carry the pressure and weight of our unhealed pain through addictions, compulsions, eating disorders, physical illness, and violence.

We are ignorant, impatient, intolerant, and desperate to hide emotions we fear through anger, control, and distractions. We create illusions about ourselves, others, and life to protect us from the original and subsequent painful truths that escalate beyond measure. We falsely believe that defenses and offenses protect us from emotional pain, instead of realizing that they create more conflict. We attack anything that threatens our walls of imprisonment, thinking the enemy is external when we have made war with ourselves.

All variations of joy and misery are inside of us. To know that we are angry, hurt, rejected, or sad, we must have experienced peace, helpfulness, acceptance, and happiness. To appreciate abundance, compassion, courage, and health, we must have experienced deprivation, suffering, fear, and sickness. These are universal feelings. When we accept and understand their arrival and departure, they are a normal part of our human experience. When we over-empower them, however, we begin a battle we can't possibly win.

When we judge and condemn certain feelings and fervently attach ourselves to the feelings of others (it's not attaching to others, only to their feelings), we suppress truth and the maturation and resolution it imparts. We endow people, places, and things with the power to produce feelings we desire and feelings we detest. Once again, we falsely believe the enemy is external, and anger and frustration intensify.

The conditions for peace are to acknowledge all that we are and all that we have done. We cannot change what we refuse to accept. We cannot meet a goal if we lack a starting point. We cannot surrender what we have not owned and understood. The machinations of ego and self-will don't amend our core life experiences, nor do they bring us serenity. Only spiritual transformation does that.

Fear of owning our pain means that the pain remains in its primitive form inside of us and the consequences of pain dominate our lives. Bullies need power over others to flee their personal demons. They cannot hold us hostage unless we ally with their fear. Whether the bully is internal or external, the solution is to practice letting go of fear. We must relinquish our weapons of judgment, hate, and vindictiveness. We must transcend our liabilities of insecurity, inferiority, and impoverishment.

Disarmament requires illumination. The power of addictions, character defects, and defenses diminishes in the presence of insight. Our self-examination must be deep and discerning. The task is to know ourselves fully and not confuse our identities or our lives with any specific feelings or experiences. Rather than fight for what we desire and fight against what we detest, we provide attention, interest, open-mindedness, patience, and time to reveal the origin and purpose of all of our feelings. This, then, precipitates a natural maturing process.

We require a thorough understanding of both our human flaws and our spiritual nature. This gives us humility, interwoven with blessedness. We are thus no longer compulsive and rigid, but spontaneous and supple. Clarity is not found in doing battle. It is discovered in stillness and quiet contemplation. Abundance does not come from greediness or grasping. It emerges from surrendering control and outcome in favor of divine purpose. The smallest light of truth shines brightly against the darkness of denial. Once we see rightly, we cannot return to blindness. No matter what our internal or external experiences, our mission is profound. We can find and take the highest ground.

....

Personal Growth Questions

1. How have I attempted to protect myself in ways that invited or reinforced more pain?
2. How have fear and judgment interfered with my healing?
3. What promotes my healing?

Affirmations

I am far greater than
painful feelings and wounds.

I can learn to process and amend harm
that I have survived.

....

How Do We Let Go?

Even when we know something's harming us and it will only get worse, it can still be a struggle to give it up. What is the process of letting go and why are certain things so hard to give up? Believing that we need a person, place, or thing in order to survive, to tolerate ourselves or our lives, or to be happy or have meaning creates dependency. Usually these needs begin when we are the most vulnerable.

Take the example of a boy who suffers repeated physical abuse from an early age and, as a teenager, discovers heroin. Not only does it magically remove all pain, it makes him feel transported to a state of bliss, comfort, and complete fulfillment. In a family that's unable to bond or show affection or interest, a child is able to adopt a pet dog. The dog allows her to feel more love than she ever imagined possible. Consider a boy who's been a social outcast all of his life, who then begins a career as a drug dealer. Suddenly, he has a surge of power, worth, and popularity. The youngest sibling in a family of bullies, who is teased for being a baby, feels adult and mature when smoking cigarettes. A girl who feels unloved at home and a failure at school discovers that boys want to be with her when she offers them sex.

As in these examples, our attachment to something can start as a protection from pain that we don't know how to manage on our own. We may not realize that we're dependent until we are threatened with the loss of our attachment. Then we may not want to get out of bed; we may have panic attacks, or cry uncontrollably, or become aggressive or willing to go against our values and morals to hold on to what we feel we need.

Even when we're not in a vulnerable, wounded place, we may try something and enjoy how it feels— smoking, shopping, eating sweets, or beginning a new friendship. If the associations we attribute to these things are powerful or numerous, a dependency can develop. Eating sweets can be associated with reward, pleasure, or giving to ourselves. A new friend can be associated with greater comfort and acceptance of ourselves. Shopping can be linked to lifting spirits. Cigarettes can be a companion when talking on the phone and driving, thereby easing stress or fortifying us before a meeting, or as an additional pleasure after sex.

Whenever we empower someone or something outside ourselves to bring us positive feelings because we have limited knowledge of how to do this for ourselves, we build dependencies that undermine our self-esteem. The more we invest in the outside for positive feelings, the less we invest in and believe in ourselves. In these circumstances, when we lose what we feel we need, it seems as if we are losing ourselves. Fear, anxiety, anger, and depression are typical emotional reactions to this kind of letting go.

If our dependencies become excessive and create significant problems, it's important to examine all dynamics underlying the dependency. This includes pain, yearnings, positive and negative associations, identity, and self-esteem. This process can involve finding support to heal pain and grieve. We can discover what we wish to have more of or less of in ourselves and our lives, and how to do that. We fully realize any negative elements and begin empowering ourselves through recognizing the positive within us. We explore who we are with greater depth and clarity, and make new associations that have healthier consequences.

The goals of the heroin addict who survived child abuse are to heal pain and create a broad support system of people who understand and have nurturing qualities. He needs to learn to set boundaries against any future abuse and develop greater compassion and appreciation for himself. He must discover natural, healthy means to mental and physical pleasures and identify and abstain from all destructive endeavors. He will process feelings about the hurtful elements of his life and grieve for what's been lost. The use of spiritual principles will help him maintain his highest core values and avoid unhealthy patterns so he can preserve positive self-esteem and nurture continuing growth.

The goals are similar for a diabetic whose sweet tooth endangers her health; or the compulsive shopper who's in severe debt; or the smoker who wants to breathe more easily and live longer; or the child whose dog dies, cutting off her only source of love; or the woman who feels empty and degraded because her only value comes from sex. All human beings long to feel good, whole, valued, and safe. We need guidance to manage pain, process feelings, and recover. When we understand ourselves fully and deeply, we can recognize our strengths and improve our weaknesses. We can choose to interact with others in ways that don't diminish them or us. We need to realize that the only things we have that can't be taken away are within us. Thus, it is our responsibility to take the healthiest care of ourselves—enjoying, learning, growing, and letting go throughout our lives.

Personal Growth Questions

1. What kinds of pain did I diminish with drugs or other compulsions?
2. What kinds of strengths did I feel when I used something compulsively?
3. What healthy tools do I use now to address and resolve pain?

Affirmations

Pain reminds me of the importance of self-care and healing.

I am increasingly growing in inner strength and faith.

Response to Fear

There's nothing inherently wrong with any emotion, including fear. However, it's important to evaluate whether our responses to fear are helpful or hurtful. When there is realistic danger, fear signals us to protect ourselves from harm, whether physical, mental, or emotional. Fear of the progressive disease of addiction and its consequences can propel us into recovery. The fear of harming our children because of parenting deficiencies can motivate us to take a parenting class or begin counseling. When we are afraid we might hurt ourselves, we can ask others to help us not act out. Fear of losing a loved one to terminal illness can cause us to draw closer and demonstrate deeper caring.

We don't always respond to fear in healthy, constructive ways, however. Real danger to some people prompts overly aggressive and provocative behaviors, which cause greater harm. Fear in addiction often triggers the use of more or stronger drugs. The fear of harming our children commonly leads to abandonment of those children to protect them from us, or demands to the children to deny their pain and fear so that we can pretend there isn't a problem. Some of us have phobias about death and dying that prevent us from visiting loved ones when they most need our support. Sometimes, we are more afraid to love and be loved than we are to hurt and be hurt.

People's thresholds for tolerating fear can be high or low, and responses vary widely, depending on prior influences and role models, especially in childhood. How significant others around us responded to fear, trauma, danger, and loss have a tremendous impact on our own responses. If we grew up with chronic chaos, crises, or abuse and the family demonstrated acceptance of these behaviors and discouraged, denied, or punished any exhibition of pain, fear, or anxiety, this defensive response can become ingrained in us as a survival tool. This is an example of high tolerance for fear. Homes where domestic violence occurs model unhealthy aggression and unhealthy passivity. Healthy assertiveness does not develop in this environment, because assertiveness arises out of self awareness, honesty, accountability, personal responsibility, and healthy boundaries. These traits are not tolerated in sick families, because they would threaten the family's defensive system, which holds the only tools they own.

Low tolerance for fear is commonly indicated by chronic anxiety, debilitating depression, and lowered ability to experience pleasure, phobias, and psychosomatic complaints. We may become overly fearful in response to mild reminders of past events that caused fear. Parents can be irrationally fearful of a child's risk of being molested at a certain age because they haven't healed from their own molestation at that age. We may attempt to control others or our environment as a response to fear of loss of internal control of emotions.

In active addiction, fear is generally responded to defensively and offensively. We may deny, drug, avoid, or minimize it, or we may act out against it through harming ourselves or others. Fear is a common precursor to violence. Fear of losing a job, security, self-esteem, pride, power, or love, for instance, can drive some people to take desperately destructive measures.

Fear of deeply examining painful past issues in recovery can keep us emotionally immature. We must be far more fearful of the disease of addiction and all that it represents than we are of committing wholeheartedly to our recovery. Addictive disease and its common companions—violence, prostitution, criminal behavior, incarceration, insanity, disease, and death—are all truly terrifying. It is also typical for addicts to have a history of equally frightening experiences prior to using. Many recovering addicts who were not afraid to face bullets in their disease are terribly afraid to face their feelings in recovery. And yet feelings are what drive addicts to use drugs. We need to re-experience our feelings in order to heal and grow beyond old beliefs and behaviors. If we haven't had healthy role models from which to learn ways to address fear, we must seek them out in recovery.

Fear increases and our effective emotional management decreases when we respond defensively and offensively to it. Whether we have a high or low tolerance to fear, we must ask ourselves if our responses help or hurt our recovery today. If our objective is to kill or diminish fear, we will fail if we try to fool ourselves. If our objective is to examine it thoroughly in order to understand it, we will arrive at a positive, constructive solution.

....

Personal Growth Questions
1. Do I have a high or low threshold for fear? What caused that?
2. What is my greatest fear and how does it impact my current life?
3. Who do I know that is a positive role model for assertiveness?

Affirmations
Past harm no longer holds me hostage.

I exchange inappropriate fear for awareness, appropriate boundaries, and understanding.

....

Stuck in Stress?

We can feel stress in our bodies. Common symptoms include strain, pain, tightness, constriction, aches, knots, churning, heaviness, unexplained drowsiness, hyperventilating, shortness of or holding our breath, loss of range of motion, and sometimes even the inability to move. It seems as if our bodies are hanging on to something and won't let go. Conversely, common physical symptoms of relaxation are release, flexibility, lightness, softness, ease, full range of motion, and a balance of inhalations and exhalations.

There are times when there is reason to be concerned and alert for danger. Often, however, we carry tension in our bodies from the past and harbor it in case we need it in the future. The physiological symptoms of stress provide effective responses to real danger. If we maintain a chronic readiness for danger, we will perceive nonstressful situations as dangerous. Thus our bodies and minds turn potential mild mishaps into major catastrophes, momentary disappointments into permanent deprivations, and positive work ethics into impossible perfectionism.

Sometimes our attitudes and beliefs promote stress. When our goals are to change others rather than ourselves, we experience stress. If we are not who we portray ourselves to be, or when outside validation is our only source of self-esteem, we experience stress. When our expectations are significantly higher or lower than what is realistic for us, we invite stress. If we overwork our bodies or minds without a balance of rest, relaxation, play, and meditation along with healthy eating and exercise, we pay a big price. When we remain attached to problems rather than process, understanding, and resolution, we refuse to grow and remain stuck in stress.

Not only do our muscles contract when we are stressed, our lives also become smaller as we are unable to acknowledge, appreciate, and invest in that which is not defined as stress. Carrying chronic or excessive tension depletes energy, exacerbates and creates health problems, narrows our choices and outlook in life, and causes us to live reactively in response to real, imagined, and potential dangers, rather than proactively in response to inner truth and spiritual principles.

The damage addiction does to the brain and body needs to be addressed in recovery. The ravages of drugs, unhealthy eating and sexual practices, recklessness, self-destructiveness, and violence create a pattern of chronic stress that requires vigorous intervention. The energy that we employ in chronic worry, doubt, and shame is the energy that we need to make amends to our physical bodies. Understanding the nature of our specific stress responses and learning how to effect positive change lets us release tension and rigidity.

Chronic stress symptoms indicate that we are stuck somewhere in our lives. We can ask ourselves questions to determine what our specific symptoms may represent. What parts of our inner or external lives are a strain or a pain and how do we change them? What feelings do we keep bottled up inside our bodies and how can we safely experience and express them? Toward what do we feel ambivalent and how can we make a decision to move forward? What are we avoiding that needs addressing? What are we afraid to say that needs to be said? What do we want that's difficult to ask for? In what ways are we punitive or withholding? What are our dreams and longings and how can we support ourselves to move toward them?

It's more difficult for our bodies to lie to us than our minds. For this reason, examining psychosomatic symptoms of stress is a valuable tool. In addition, taking cues from the body's natural responses to relaxation can direct our improvements. Therapeutic massages often unblock emotional pain and memories, allowing us an opportunity to begin healing in these areas. When we take a break from working on a problem and let ourselves relax, solutions are more likely to occur to us. We can explore what triggers hope, positive self-esteem, ease, and balance. This, in turn, allows us to view a larger perspective and have more options. These are positive triggers that we need in our lives on a daily basis.

Just as our bodies need to balance inhalations and exhalations, our lives need a balance between receiving and giving. When we seek only to take from others and our environment, we are stressed. When we fail to provide for our own welfare first and give only to others, we are stressed. People, places, behaviors, and emotions that reinforce stress need to be identified so that we can contemplate healthier responses, including detachment. This is a process that requires focused attention, work, time, and often assistance from others. Let's make this a part of our daily inventory.

....

Personal Growth Questions

1. What are my symptoms of stress physically, mentally, and emotionally?
2. What are the ways in which I can make amends to my body?
3. Answer the questions asked on pages 67-68.

Affirmations

I agree to identify and practice solutions for stress on a daily basis.

Serenity is increasingly comfortable, familiar, and enjoyable to me.

....

Pleasure and Pain in Recovery

It is in our nature to seek pleasurable and rewarding states. When we live in an environment that chronically fails to meet our primary psychological needs or does not support healthy growth and fulfillment, we look for other means to experience a sense of pleasure and reward. When our honest, vulnerable expressions encounter repeated rejection, our real selves—with our genuine needs, wants, thoughts, and feelings— go underground. We refocus attention on what works best for us in an unhealthy environment. Primary needs are given up for secondary gains. This means that our worlds begin to feel smaller. Since secondary goals can never compensate for primary needs, we increasingly experience constriction, oppression, and frustration. Defenses attempt to dull awareness of the pain from our losses.

When our need for a safe, secure, nurturing experience is not met sufficiently, we are vulnerable to idealizing isolation and recklessness, or to seeking a drugged state that numbs emotional pain and allows us to feel pleasure. Or we may overfeed ourselves to stimulate the sense of reward, and then deaden these feelings by overloading our systems. We may seek relationships where need and rejection, or passive or aggressive codependency, are re-enacted. We may become phobic and controlling in an attempt to create safety and comfort.

If our unique strengths and talents are not observed or valued, if our innate personalities are not appreciated or understood, if our feelings and thoughts have no impact, if we're not seen for who we are, but only for what someone wishes us to be, then these issues repeat in our lives over and over. We may, as a consequence, suffer low self-esteem or pursue goals for another rather than what is best for us. We may become overly opinion-ated, bullying, manipulative, or preachy in an attempt to compensate for the reverse situations earlier in our lives. We may do things to deaden ourselves further from who we really are and what we truly want, just to offset the pain. We may impose our needs and yearnings on others or pretend to be different than we really are to win acceptance.

We internalize our primary role models in childhood. When they are unhealthy, we find ourselves stuck in internal and external struggles that reflect our caretakers' themes. If anger, abandonment, control, compulsions, depression, disappointment, or deprivation were our caretakers' struggles, there's a very good chance that they will also be ours. So how do we let go of patterns adopted from environments that couldn't tolerate vulnerability and honesty?

We are powerless to change negative circumstances that face us as long as we keep looking in the same direction. We are stuck when we are afraid to see how we got somewhere and when we are afraid to re-experience the pain that resulted in our present dilemmas. The solution is to fear the complete death of our real selves and real lives more than we fear facing the pain of our journey without defenses. Our eyes and hearts must be wide open in self-examination. We need to reawaken our sensitivity and vulnerability to pain so that we can suspend our dispensing of it to ourselves and others. We must revisit our primary psychological needs and let go of our attachments to secondary defensive gains. We need to tear down walls we built against our understanding if we are ever to achieve healthy intimacy.

Mature love for ourselves and others is based on deep understanding, not control, dependency, or apathy. Our real selves always know our true desires, needs, feelings, thoughts, and purpose. We need to return to who we were before we began the deception of pretending, defending, and denying. At one time, we were fully alive and real, moment to moment. In order to reclaim our truth, we must face the pain of its rejection again and not erect defenses. We must stand firm in support of our highest good.

We need to provide for ourselves and allow others to help us develop an enriching, encouraging, and challenging environment for actualizing our genuine selves and building lives that evolve from their own unfolding. We could not do this earlier in our lives. It is recovery that gives us the opportunity to reach our greatest happiness, serenity, and fulfillment, and to share it with others. Healthy pleasure and reward come from our ability to embrace our highest inner truths and grow from our pain.

....

Personal Growth Questions
1. What were my most important primary needs that were not met in childhood?
2. What secondary gains or defenses did I adopt as a result of unmet needs?
3. How do I, or can I, fulfill an important primary need currently?

Affirmations

I have the strength today to release
my defenses and reclaim my truth.

I accept responsibility for creating a healthy
environment and support system, and
I enjoy mutually rewarding relationships.

....

Mistaken Beliefs

To be hurt when we are powerless to protect ourselves, to be unable to understand, and to have no tools for resolution, negatively impacts how we see ourselves and our lives. When we are wounded by someone's sickness, we receive not only the pain and consequences of the wound, but the wounder's way of thinking. So now we not only carry pain that we don't know how to heal, but we accept a belief system that ensures continued pain.

We may then hurt ourselves, because we think that this is what we deserve. Or we may act out as a cry for help, or because the pain is so great that we wish to die. We may hurt others, believing this will rid us of our own pain. If certain people remind us of those who have hurt us, we may misplace retribution on them. We can become aggressive because it makes us feel powerful and hides our painful vulnerability, or because we think that the only way to prevent further hurt is to adopt the opposing role. We can allow or encourage others to hurt us because we accept our wounder's projected view of us. Perhaps we associate love with control, possession, and powerful need. We may believe that our only other option is to be alone and that we are our own worst enemies. Or we may fear the unknown far more than painful familiarity.

Once we let go of our addictions and compulsions, we still have faulty thinking. Present problems can restimulate feelings from similar past problems and trigger scenarios of potential future problems. Thus our pain, anger, and other reactions to current conflicts represent a significant overreaction. When we can't separate current from past or potential future problems, we are powerless to find an effective solution. When we cannot distinguish our own identities from our false selves or from others' beliefs and identities, we feel overwhelmingly negative about ourselves, others, and our lives. This entanglement takes from us the energy that we need to move forward in life and keeps us merely struggling to survive.

We are afraid to surrender our tools of survival, forgetting that these tools arose from confusion, despair, fear, horror, and rage. Obviously, these mental states were not conducive to the development of healthy solutions. Additionally, our first experiences of being hurt are usually in childhood when we lack knowledge, options, a variety of support, and control over what happens to us. As time goes on, we fail to see how our expectations, assumptions, beliefs, and reactions compel us to repeat toxic patterns. Instead, we think life is reinforcing our original negative beliefs and we cling ever more tightly to defensive counter-measures against anything or anyone that remotely reminds us of our original suffering. We think we've got reality figured out, yet we perpetually manifest mistaken beliefs, which halt healing, learning, and growth.

Twelve-step work directs us to correct these faulty patterns with a paradoxical solution. We are powerless when victimized, thus we think our problem is powerlessness, and we struggle against it. Instead, we must learn to discern and accept the areas where we have power and the areas where we do not. We are powerless over the past and future, and denying this perpetuates guilt and worry. We are powerless over people, places, and things, and the more we obsess over them, the more angry and frustrated we feel.

We not only have power, but a responsibility, to put recovery first, to become and remain spiritually fit, to practice honesty and depth in self-reflection, to assist others without thought of personal gain, and to cause no further harm to ourselves or others. We must confront and correct within us the consequences and symptoms of harm. Healing is the gradual experiencing of compassion over judgment, understanding over vengeance, and love over fear and hate. We must first have these experiences for ourselves. It is only then that we can genuinely and fully give them to others. When other people remain harmful, we must love ourselves enough to keep them close in our prayers and distant from our presence. We must keep the people with whom we share healthy reciprocal love near to us, whether they are physically present, distant, or departed.

We are challenged by abandonment, abuse, disease, false indoctrination, impoverishment, injustice, loss, trauma, and war. To be healed means that we've exchanged the mistaken beliefs arising from challenges, for personal responsibility in our recovery. We amend the harm we caused others and mend the harm that others caused us. Our frame of reference is no longer how others treated us, but how our Higher Power wishes us to treat ourselves and others. Our vision today tells us how much pain exists in life, how we are all interconnected, and how only beliefs and behaviors born of divine love can make it bearable and bring blessings back into life.

....

Personal Growth Questions
1. What are the areas in which my thinking remains faulty?
2. How does my faulty thinking impact my life and my self-esteem?
3. What would be healthy thinking in these areas?

Affirmations
I allow the spiritual principles of recovery to direct my decisions and actions today.

I release mistaken beliefs and create new concepts based on compassion and understanding.

....

Grace Lost and Found

Recovery from Abuse

Unfortunately, it is common for people with addictive disease to have significant physical and sexual abuse histories, particularly in childhood. Steps four and five in the 12-step program provide an opportunity to disclose these experiences, feelings, and consequences, and to be listened to with compassion and understanding. This alone, however, is rarely sufficient to heal the damage from severe abuse.

Typical symptoms of survivors include phobias, difficulties with trust and control, significant memory loss, emotional insulation, dissociation, destructive addictions and compulsions (including eating disorders), strong fears of intimacy and vulnerability, negative self-image, acting out sexually or physically or attracting partners who do so, and chronic, intense states of anger, shame, fear, and depression. Abuse in childhood severely handicaps our ability to further develop psychologically.

Abuse damages our sense of safety, especially when no one responds empathetically and protectively on our behalf. As children, we are dependent upon our caretakers to meet our physical and psychological needs. If, instead, we are forced to meet the sick needs of others or we receive harm instead of nurturing, we internalize this lack of safety and have profound problems with trust. And because we are children, we believe it is our fault.

Autonomy is damaged, because abuse violates the boundaries that establish basic personal rights and individual separation from others. Personal rights include appropriate privacy and the ability to communicate our own needs, wants, thoughts, and feelings, and to receive respect and consideration for them. When our caretakers chronically override our needs and feelings in childhood, we feel overly responsible for ourselves and our families. We cannot separate ourselves from them, or our feelings and needs from theirs. This leads to overwhelming pain and feelings of failure.

True identity development cannot take place without autonomy. Personal identity, instead, is comprised of the internalization of the abuser's projections and our response to them. We are thus unable to see ourselves as whole or capable, and our abilities for self-caretaking are severely compromised. We come to know ourselves deeply when afforded time and encouragement for self-reflection, exploration, and trial and error to determine our strengths, weaknesses, talents, interests, life philosophy, purpose, and spirituality. We cannot discover who we truly are and what best serves us on our unique paths in life when others' impositions dominate this process.

When our social environment is healthy, it provides accurate observations and validation for our unique personalities. This lays the groundwork for healthy empowerment and a proactive, assertive approach to life. When a healthy set of beliefs, values, and priorities evolve from deep personal examination and understanding, and when our behavior is in accord with them, we have positive self-esteem. This is obviously lacking in survivors who were abused in childhood or early adolescence.

When our bodies have been invaded and violently attacked, healthy valuing and caretaking of our physical selves is usually poor. Neglect, self-mutilation, recklessness, self-destructiveness, eating disorders, drug abuse, prostitution, and ongoing abusive relationships further endanger health and life in abuse survivors. At the same time, dissociating, numbing physical pain, and using substances to promote the illusion of pleasure rather than pain are common defenses against horror and tragedy.

Our idea of a power greater than ourselves begins in childhood, with our parents or other caretakers as role models. When these role models are unhealthy, our spiritual views are tainted with cruelty, unrealistic standards for conditional acceptance, punitive self-sacrifice, a deep sense of being unlovable, unworthiness, and rejection. This creates a tenuous struggle between life and death.

When, instead of healthy love, we receive attacks on our bodies and spirits, fear overpowers love. There is a desperate striving to overcome emptiness and an equal amount of fear with vulnerability and intimacy. The emptiness is the ache of severe deprivation trying to get our attention. The past tells us, however, that the yearning for bonding and nurturing will only bring violence, enmeshment, and suffocation.

For healing to begin, we must discuss the abuse we suffered, until we discover all that we internalized that inhibits our recovery today. What thoughts, values, feelings, and behaviors are linked to projections of abusers that we absorbed as our own? Our health today relies on separating ourselves from sick internalizations and people who are toxic to us. We must return to our original needs, wants, feelings, and thoughts, and give them respect and consideration. We need to learn and practice healthy caretaking, valuing, and compassionate confrontation with ourselves. We are responsible for keeping ourselves safe and for giving time to personal reflection to discover our true identities. Our spiritual relationships will then change to reflect the healthy relationships we are building with ourselves and others in recovery. This teaches us how love overpowers fear.

....

Personal Growth Questions

1. What symptoms and consequences do I experience as a result of past abuse?
2. What kind of people and situations stimulate distrust and fear in me? How do I respond to this?
3. What healthy boundaries and responses would I like to develop to promote my healing?

Affirmations

I am learning to give myself positive attention, respect, value, and unconditional love.

I am willing to protect myself from harm and nurture my health and happiness.

....

Grace Lost and Found

Proactive or Reactive?

Negative actions are typically misguided attempts to fix very real problems. Prostitution symbolizes a need to value, validate, and attend to the sexual part of self to heal past wounds. Stealing is an attempt to rectify earlier important deprivations. Self-mutilation is a need to kill vulnerability in order to kill the fear of its consequences. Substance abuse comes from the need to control what enters the mind and body in response to previous painful internalizations. Violence represents a need to communicate the origin of rage and consequent feelings of victimization.

When we haven't learned tools that help us reach solutions, we act out our pain in ways that do further harm to ourselves and others. Therefore prostitution, stealing, self-mutilation, substance abuse, and violence give more power to the people and experiences that brought on our original pain. We become reactive rather than proactive, and remain stuck in sick behaviors and ideas. We are afraid to examine the dynamics of negative behavior, ironically because we believe it will reinforce it. Yet it is only truth in its entirety that will free us from the bondage of old habits.

Arresting negative actions is the first stage of recovery. Generally, what motivates us to stop problematic behaviors is that we can no longer deny the escalating pain that they bring, and we've managed to maintain a small part of ourselves that feels that we are worthy of and can benefit from assistance. We cannot pretend to be in charge of our lives when harmful actions are the power greater than ourselves.

This is a stage of recovery in which we typically need significant support to reinforce change, to provide healthier sources of Higher Power, and to increase hope. Ideally, as we let go of old sick behaviors, we internalize new concepts of relating to ourselves and others. It is more difficult to let go of internalized belief systems and their corresponding emotions, however, than it is to change the outward behaviors.

A conscious, focused exploration of the genesis of negative actions in order to understand and heal the wounds below them is the second stage of recovery. When core problems begin in childhood, our early examinations of them in recovery trigger the feelings and thoughts experienced at that age. We feel helpless, hopeless, vulnerable, terrified, and overwhelmed. We think we are undeserving of healthy affection, attention, love, nurturing, protection, support, and value. We believe that there is something inherently wrong with our intelligence, our abilities, our bodies, our feelings, our needs, our wants, our love, and our right to live. Failing to address or complete this part of recovery leaves us with barriers to healthy intimacy with ourselves, with others, and with the God of our understanding.

Recovery in the second stage requires healing and understanding on the physical, mental, emotional, spiritual, and behavioral levels. For instance, if prostitution developed from unhealed sexual abuse, once it stops, an analysis of the myriad symptoms and consequences that followed from sexual abuse other than prostitution is in order. Physically, the body may be treated as a function, tool, or curse. Mentally, sex may be viewed as repulsive, with accompanying thoughts of suicide, self-hate, and self-doubt. Emotionally, chronic shame, guilt, anger, fear, and anxiety interfere with self-esteem. Spiritually, the Higher Power may be understood as unforgiving, punishing, uncaring, or neglectful. Behaviorally, deficient self-care in terms of health, boundaries, safety, and relationships are typical symptoms, as well as a need for perfection to compensate for negative thoughts about self.

The above examples only scratch the surface of the work needed in this area. Talking about problems, past and present, with trustworthy, understanding people can stimulate positive change. When we see how these problems and consequent symptoms stem from sickness, we understand how we've been reacting from fear and false beliefs. These beliefs limit or prevent us from fully receiving or giving attention, affection, bonding, empathy, love, and understanding. If we believe, ultimately, that the true source of our lives comes from a healthy, loving Higher Power, then we know confidently that we are far greater than the sum of any traumas given or received. We deserve healing and growth on every level. This is what allows us to live proactively rather than reactively. The depth of the darkness we face and reconcile within ourselves determines the power of spiritual illumination for our lives.

Personal Growth Questions

1. In what ways am I proactive and in what areas am I reactive in my current life?
2. What changes can I make in action, thought, or feeling to become more proactive?
3. What are my ideal goals for myself physically, mentally, emotionally, spiritually, and behaviorally?

Affirmations

I am transforming past unhealthy patterns into character strengths.

As my personal understanding broadens and deepens, so does my capacity to create for my highest good.

Chapter 3

Relationships with Self, Others, and a Higher Power

WHEN WE HAVEN'T HAD EXAMPLES of healthy, mature love, we end up using or being used by people. We see love as a function or a fix rather than a full, reciprocal relationship. We see love as something that completes, dominates, or submits to us rather than enhances us. We wish to feel as if we love and are loved, but our desperate and perennial striving to be one step ahead of emptiness indicates otherwise. When we are excited but have no peace, when we yearn but lack acceptance or are satiated from without rather than within, we are not experiencing loving feelings.

If we demand attention by monopolizing or by having the last or loudest words, we have received nothing of internal value. If we seek safety in over-controlling our partners, we're not safe with ourselves. If we're apathetic in order not to be hurt by our loved ones, we're giving past hurts the power to keep us wounded. If we attempt to buy love through money or excessive one-sided giving, all that we receive is a deepened sense of unworthiness. When we feel we've failed to secure our needs for love, we may turn to the opposite extreme and act recklessly or violently, or be passive or submissive. Or we may isolate ourselves from people and seek love through food, drugs, shopping, or other compulsions.

That Loving Feeling

If we don't know what healthy love is, how do we develop it? The suggestion of 12-step programs to avoid entering a relationship in early recovery is an excellent one. Romantic relationships bring forth all the elements of our past unresolved conflicts and wounds. In early sobriety, we have no tools to address this. We lack an honest and deep understanding of ourselves, as well as self-esteem. We are still driven by our defenses, character defects, and negative internalizations. We can't differentiate between the devious and powerful influence of the disease and the healthy parts of our minds, and we are hungry for a fix to avoid all this painful work.

Not only can premature relationships trigger relapse, they also prevent us from creating a new foundation inside ourselves that lets us attract and participate in mature relationships. When we fix on anyone or anything, we reinforce an inner lack of wholeness; we give anxiety and pain dominance over the person we are; we fail to see our Higher Power within us. Fixes are a fear response to inner pain and problems. We cannot take our inventory and practice spiritual principles while we are still running away. All of our pain and problems deserve to be transformed. All of our strengths and talents deserve to be developed and practiced.

Twelve-step programs promise us blessings and miracles. They help us to recognize what harms us and what helps us. We are asked to identify a healthy power greater than ourselves that can direct our recovery to our highest good. The program doesn't judge, discriminate, coerce, or condemn, nor does it abandon anyone. We are told that, when we stray from spiritual principles, our lives become unmanageable. If we are not convinced, we are invited to continue to use our will to lead us until we realize it is willingness, not willfulness that gives us freedom from harm. The tools and support of recovery are freely given. It is always our choice whether to use them. When we share the pain of our past and present circumstances, there are people to help us accept, understand, and work toward responsible solutions. This is how pain is transformed; it is redefined as a part of our life experience that requires healing; it ceases being what identifies us, defines our lives, or overpowers us.

Our relationship with these programs may well be our first experience with mature love and it is a beautiful blueprint. Many of us feel our Higher Power gives us free will, unconditional love, and guidance toward recognizing and achieving our fullest and highest potential. When we believe we are created from this power, it means we are created from love. No matter how far we stray as imperfect human beings in an imperfect world, there is a spiritual part of us that is perfect. Our willingness to be inspired and directed by our Higher Power can lead us to experience new heights and depths of loving feelings. The ability to help ourselves and others in positive ways, and the ability to give and receive mature love, depends on the quality of our conscious contact with the ultimate source and wellspring of love.

....

Personal Growth Questions

1. What are my examples of immature loving?
2. What character traits need further development for me to demonstrate healthier love?
3. What substitutes for love have I turned to in the past?

Affirmations

I am so much more than
my mind can imagine.

Through the spirit of love,
we bring Heaven to earth.

....

Your Childhood Holds the Key to Love

Twelve-step programs tell us that we can't give away what we don't have. If we wish to give and receive healthy, mature love, then we need to find it first within ourselves. The primary model for love comes from how we felt loved or unloved as children and how love was demonstrated in our families. Additionally, the objects, activities, experiences, places, animals, and people that we loved most as children are the keys to loving ourselves today.

Characteristics commonly seen in children who reside in healthy environments are heightened hope, energy, comfort, confidence, curiosity, creativity, spontaneity, awe, wonder, and idealization. These characteristics are often present at all ages in the honeymoon stage of love. When we've experienced sufficient hardship, disappointment, hurt, or trauma, we can lose many or all of these traits. Reclaiming them, with the exception of idealization, is one of the goals of developing healthy love.

Idealization magnifies or fabricates positive elements and denies or minimizes negative elements. Therefore, it keeps us from seeing what is real. Mature love is based on true, deep understanding of ourselves and our partners. Idealization is a fantasy based on our needs and a false belief that a partner will rescue us from harm and provide only positive experiences for us. Thus, one of the tasks of adulthood is seeing and accepting ourselves, others, and the world as whole with both positive and negative aspects.

Another reason why, as adults, we must love ourselves first to love others is to learn primary responsibility for our own healing, caretaking, and growth. We see how it is not magical and easy, but requires deep conscious awareness. It is difficult to heal, recover, and grow from hurtful experiences. Accepting this responsibility allows us to see others as they are, rather than as we selfishly wish them to be. Learning to love our whole selves and committing to become the best that we can be allows us to love others and commit to a working partnership.

The character traits of integrity, honesty, understanding, attentiveness, and autonomy are essential to healthy, mature love. When a person's words and behavior match their feelings, energy, motivation, body language, tone, and attitude, there is integrity. When the outward doesn't match the inward, the internal communication is dominant.

For example, if I tell my partner I'm happy and nothing's wrong, and my partner senses I'm tense, withdrawn, and have no energy, my partner understandably gives credence to the internal message.

So if we pretend to be in a positive place with ourselves and the truth is that we chronically battle self-hate, self-doubt, and unworthiness, once the idealization stage is over, the relationship will mirror our real inner state. Our partners relate to, interact with, and reflect back to us our internal communication, which is based on our real feelings toward ourselves.

If our goal is to experience reciprocal, healthy, mature love, we must look at our childhoods. Childhood holds the keys to our original beliefs about love, ourselves, and experiences that triggered love. We reexamine old beliefs to process, change, understand, and edit out what is unhealthy and further develop what is healthy.

We are responsible for healing our wounds and creating conditions conducive to our happiness and well-being. We make positive use of our Higher Power, support systems, and, often, counselors, to do so. We must experience in ourselves the same unbounded joy that a healthy parent feels for their child. When we identify character defects, we must examine ourselves to understand them and work toward solutions, rather than condemn and punish ourselves. We inventory the parts of our world and ourselves in childhood that triggered intense absorption, interest, comfort, happiness, excitement, creativity, and growth. We find healthy ways to incorporate them into who we are and what our lives are today.

There are people in recovery who emphasize amending harm done to others over harm done to self. There are others who emphasize harm done to themselves over harm to others. We need to address both equally. We need to see what we like and don't like, what is healthy and what is sick, what is weak and what is strong to truly understand and to make positive changes. This is part of learning mature, healthy love. There are no fixes and this doesn't come quickly or easily. We must rely on patience, tolerance, and faith to keep us on a path toward healthier love. When we love ourselves in the healthiest sense, we have a never-ending supply of love for others as well.

Personal Growth Questions

1. What did I learn about love in my childhood?
2. How do I demonstrate healthy love? How do I demonstrate lack of love or unhealthy love?
3. What do I need to heal in myself in order to surrender self-defeating behaviors?

Affirmations

I grow beyond my past by learning important lessons and focusing on present solutions.

I practice the elements of healthy self-love on a daily basis.

Repairing Relationships

The disease of addiction gratifies sick, destructive needs. Healthy needs of self and others are increasingly ignored. This is part of the defensive self-centeredness of the active addict. The solution in sobriety is to cultivate compassion, honesty, sensitivity, and respect, and to demonstrate this through service to others. Ultimately and ironically, however, we must also become self-centered again—but in a healthy, constructive manner. Our deepest core selves are connected to our Higher Power. As we use recovery to let go of defensive, destructive needs, and create an environment that supports healthy needs as well as our strengths and talents, we honor our real selves as a gift from our Higher Power.

Active addiction harms self and others physically, mentally, emotionally, and spiritually. This means that a full amends to self and others is in order for complete recovery. We must identify specific ways that we harmed ourselves and others in our adolescence and adulthood. We do not hold ourselves responsible for harm given or received in childhood, however. Children internalize, imitate, and act from the role models in their environment. When children are harmful, it is either because there is damage to the brain or, more commonly, it is a reaction to how they have been harmed in some way. When children are abused, abandoned, or deprived of normal, healthy physical and psychological needs, the damage is never their fault.

Amends to others entail an accounting of specific harm remembered by the addict, an invitation to others to relate any additional harm that they recall, and a dialogue regarding feelings and thoughts about the incidents. The addict's demonstration of positive attitude and behavior changes must accompany this experience and continue in future encounters. The changes correct past unhealthy behaviors so that no new harm is perpetrated. Some significant others have unrealistic or unhealthy expectations of amends. They may think the recovering person is supposed to meet their every desire and need, never hurting their feelings or disappointing them again. They mistakenly believe this control over the addict will make up for constraints and deprivations suffered from the disease. Some significant others feel they should be able to harm, mistreat, or exploit the addict in retaliation for the abuse that they sustained. These ideas are not healthy for either party and do not correct past problems.

Amends to self entail an accounting of beliefs, feelings, and actions that harmed us. This includes the damaging internalizations initiated by others. Addicts who survived traumas deserve to heal from the traumas themselves, as well as from their reactions or retaliations. When character defects stem from childhood wounds, this identification is an important part of releasing them. For instance, if we are cruel, we were denied compassion; if we are impulsive, our emotions were not contained; if we are destructive, we were not kept safe. Children who are significantly harmed falsely believe they are at fault. This belief attracts others who perpetuate similar harm and trigger self-abuse. Recovering addicts must alter their self-image to facilitate a new relationship with self, based on recovery principles. Healing, insight, and growth must replace toxic punishment and repetition of harm.

When recovering addicts make amends to those who abused them, it is ideal if they have first made amends to themselves in this area. Otherwise, there is a possibility of the addict feeling re-wounded by these persons. If the addict has healed in the area of the original harm, any possible toxic response on the part of others who have not healed or grown themselves will be minimized. In general, the more insight we've gained and the more healthy changes we've made, the more our amends will have a positive impact for all.

When we are not healthy, we see ourselves and others through gross distortions. When we deny our real thoughts, feelings, and behaviors in response to drugs, or in response to others who impose their needs upon us, we deny ourselves the very love that we need to grow, and the conscious awareness of the spiritual connection that sustains us. We do this to others as well. When I judge and condemn myself harshly, remain angry or frenetic to avoid vulnerability, hide the parts of myself that I fear, torment myself with unrealistic expectations, pretend I am apathetic and stoic in response to hurt, then I cannot see you or me. I only see what is artificially contrived from fear. We can't give away what we don't have and we can't receive love that we don't feel for ourselves. We can repeat what is sick in our relationships with ourselves and others, or we can realize that we deserve healing and that it begins with us.

....

Personal Growth Questions

1. What is the most significant harm I have done to myself and others?
2. What changes in my thinking and behaviors will prepare me for the amends process?
3. What standards and boundaries can I develop to improve my relations with others?

*I abstain from harming anyone and
demonstrate helping and healing today.*

*I replace anger, blame, and
fear with understanding,
self-examination, and compassion.*

Love without Fear

Much of what is written about love is not really about
love, but rather about myriad obstacles to love. Addiction, blame, defects, and defenses block love. Healthy,
mature love places spiritual values first. This is only
possible when we've completed a deep, thorough self-
examination and personal growth process. Our authentic selves must emerge and take full responsibility
for our well-being and ongoing development. Appreciation, compassion, honesty, integrity, joy, laughter,
patience, peace, tolerance, respect, and understanding dominate actions, feelings, and thoughts in mature
loving relationships.

The original source of love is our Higher Power.
Therefore, love arises from the highest part of ourselves and sees the highest in others. Divine love flows
through us continuously. There is no possibility of being deprived of, or depleting, love. When we feel or
think that this is so, it is because we have over-focused
on painful experiences with others where love was

blocked, and this diminished our conscious awareness of our spiritual truth. Our associations to love come from our human experience, which is then often projected onto our Higher Power.

Chronic feelings of aloneness, brokenness, cravings, emptiness, and neediness also indicate an over-investment in the false self that's created in reaction to painful experiences. All of these fear-based feelings trigger regression to less-developed mental states and behaviors. This holds us hostage to recreating and repeating similar scenarios. And so we remain short-sighted and misguided. Our awareness of love withers away in the presence of fear, as does our potential for personal growth.

Real love can't be controlled or fashioned from expectations and plans. It is unbroken, unconditional, and unending. Love has no needs, only desire. It doesn't intrude or impose, but will inspire us when we welcome it. It does not absorb or deliver harm, for it sees harm as fear in action, and love has no fear. Love is affectionate, attentive, considerate, creative, patient, playful, surprising, transforming, and understanding. Love's energy is free, healing, and perennially positive.

Obstacles to love exist because we believe they protect us from harm. Defenses and adaptations arise when we experience hurt and have no healthy modeling or assistance to understand, take care of ourselves and/or the problem, and allow the pain to depart. Without this healing process, each time a new hurt is experienced, defenses become stronger. They can eventually close off our hearts.

To recall our openness to love, we need to think of an interaction with an animal, person, or place in which we felt at peace, yet wonderfully energized and blissfully absorbed in the moment. (This does not include drugged states.) Generally, it's easier for us to allow love to emerge when we feel safe with the subject or object. It's then helpful to practice experiencing "safe" loving moments, so that they become more familiar and dominant in our lives.

When we wish to surrender old defensive protections that close our hearts, we can investigate our specific triggers for pain and fear. We need to determine the differences between current triggers and those that were present in childhood. When we are immersed in an unhealthy lifestyle—from addictions, compulsions, codependencies, or other negative-thinking-based behaviors—we may not see much difference. In this case, the negative pattern must be disrupted through a significant period of treatment, before disparities emerge.

Following a lengthy abstinence from unhealthy patterns and participation in personal awareness and growth, clear differences can be perceived between experiences stimulating current fear and those that generated fear in childhood. There are innumerable associations to painful events. Until we heal emotionally, any association—including minor and peripheral ones—can activate the full pain of the original event and its consequent defensiveness or offensiveness.

Once we establish a new foundation of healthy patterns, we can terminate these automatic regressions. We remind ourselves that we are now adults capable of creating safety, using positive resources, setting appropriate boundaries, and communicating assertively. We can ascertain which part of a hurtful interchange is our responsibility to resolve and which is not. Once we know and understand ourselves deeply, we have greater patience, tolerance, and understanding of human dynamics in general. This frees us from internalizing and reacting defensively or offensively to others. This is the work that allows us to keep our hearts open to loving those we wish to love—whether that is spiritual, familial, friendly, or romantic love.

We are not helpless children, dependent upon how others treat us for our well-being and survival. We are self-reliant adults who choose the level and frequency of participation with others. We do this according to what allows us to maintain self-respect, self-esteem, and integrity, yet challenges us to continue learning and maturing. Additionally, worries about our welfare diminish appreciably as our relationship with our God deepens. The more confident we become in our faith and in our ability to take healthy care of ourselves, the more our hearts remain open to love. And love is the grandest expression of the divine.

Personal Growth Questions

1. What behaviors, emotions, and thoughts block me from experiencing love?
2. With whom or what have I experienced healthy, unconditional love? Discuss the experience.
3. What is one event in childhood that triggered my defensiveness concerning love.

Affirmations

I am worthy of unconditional love, respect, and understanding.

Demonstrating spiritual principles in my relationship with self allows me to participate in healthy relations with others.

Recovery from Loss

Loss of someone important typically triggers some abandonment of ourselves, as well as depression. The more we have invested energy, focus, goals, love, and time in another, the more we can feel empty after their loss. This commonly decreases our desire, energy, interest, and motivation in life. Self-caretaking, nurturing, and attention to responsibilities may diminish considerably, especially in the early stages of grief. We may not wish to continue our efforts, endeavors, or even our lives. And yet a sense of duty and habit generally prevail, and we walk through normal behaviors with significantly less than full engagement and presence.

In healthy relationships, we maintain autonomy and identity. This means that—no matter how much we have in common with our loved ones, how deep the bond and how long we have been together—we are unique individuals with an understanding and investment in ourselves, our life purpose, and our path. The greater our emotional and mental health, the more our inner truths and values align with outward behavior and communication. This gives us inner strength and resilience. Loss is painful, but more tolerable because we have a whole sense of identity.

When we lack the psychological development for true autonomy and identity, loss and grief will either be far more traumatic or will not be experienced deeply in a conscious manner. The latter can occur if we've failed to bond significantly in the first place. The former may occur as a result of having nothing to fall back on when the loved one is gone. Without a true sense of self, we become part of our loved one's identity. Loss then seems to threaten our very existence and self-destructive behavior may ensue.

Common grief reactions include eating or sleeping too much or too little, numbing or overwhelming feelings, distracting and anxiety-based over-activity or significant under-activity, and intense preoccupation with or defensive avoidance of loss. Feelings of anger, anxiety, confusion, emptiness, and sadness are typical. We may also question our purpose, the meaning of love and life, and our understanding of God. Our unique personalities, emotional strengths, maturity, resources, spiritual beliefs and practices, and the nature of the specific loss will all affect how grieving proceeds.

It is normal to feel less equilibrium when our lives change profoundly. It's important to discuss our feelings and thoughts, and the consequences of our loss with people who understand this process. Deep emotional and mental exploration is best done with others who are comfortable and productive with their own intensive process efforts. This helps us feel safe to expose our vulnerability. It takes time to address the levels of responses to loss and to readjust our lives. Therefore, we need to apply patience and tolerance to this work.

There are three elements to identify and understand in bereavement—the positive, the negative, and the fantasy parts of the relationship and their effect on us. We can experience gratitude for and continue to honor the positive aspects by maintaining those qualities or their meaning in some fashion in our lives. We can examine any negative parts of the relationship to see what inside of us needs healing and maturing. In other words, what part of us attracted and participated in negative attitudes or behaviors and how can we apply recovery tools to transform these elements? It's also natural to have wished for relationship improvements and, especially if the relationship was rewarding, to have hoped that it would last forever. These wishes may have changed into beliefs or expectations. If this occurred, there may be a strong attachment to the fantasy, which denies the reality of the bond and complicates the grief process.

The clarity and quality of our connections determine the clarity and quality of our lives, because all of life is interconnected. Allowing ourselves to walk honestly and openly through our feelings in response to loss creates a climate conducive to healing and growth. Chronically attempting to protect ourselves from this process increases the loss. Protecting brings more pain, more denial and despair, and more negativity into our lives. When we fail to invest in ourselves honestly and fully, we curtail our ability to give and receive, and loss of intimacy becomes pervasive. Understanding the depth and meaning of our bonds with our loved ones emotionally, mentally, physically, and spiritually greatly increases our understanding of ourselves and of our specific needs in ongoing recovery. Opening our hearts when they are full of pain in order to heal, and opening to the confusion in our minds in order to question and expand our beliefs reinforces intimacy. Recovery from loss ultimately allows us to grow in our ability to love ourselves, others, life, and God.

....

Personal Growth Questions
1. How have I behaviorally, emotionally, and mentally responded to loss?
2. How has loss affected my relationship with myself and others?
3. What have I learned from loss that helps me grow psychologically and spiritually?

Affirmations
My life improves, not through my will, but
through my openness to learning and growth.

My understanding of loss ultimately
deepens my demonstration of love.

....

Domestic Violence and Addiction

Abusers in domestic-violence relationships are typically jealous, possessive, distrustful, deceptive, manipulative, and controlling. They are emotionally, mentally, and/or physically violent. They have irrational rigid thinking, and are easily frustrated and overwhelmed. Abusers are unable to contain troubling emotions and blame their partners for their own pain. They relate to their partners only as a function for their own needs. Any part of the significant others' lives that threatens the abusers' need for control is disempowered or removed. Abusers ultimately seek total domination over their partners.

In the early part of a relationship with an abuser, they typically exhibit charm, generosity, financial investment, over-involvement, and an excessive amount of interest, time, and affection. However, the needs, wants, and personal information of their partners are only sought, attended to, and valued for the purpose of control and to foster attraction and dependency toward the abuser. Promises are implied or verbalized by the abuser for ulterior motives. A quick dependency and a speedy progression from attraction to sex is sought, because this indicates the significant other is in familiar territory and will likely participate longer in an unhealthy relationship.

Once the partner is sufficiently dependent upon the abuser, the partner's needs, wants, thoughts, and feelings can be ignored and gratification can be withheld purposefully to punish. Abusers typically believe that others' gratification diminishes theirs. The significant other's role is to satisfy the increasing needs and wants of the abuser in spite of the abuser's inability to experience fulfillment when this is accomplished. The abuser's needs can never be met in reality, because they are meant to "fix" an inside problem that no partner can ever repair. The significant other is the container for the rage experienced by the abuser in earlier experiences in which he or she was mistreated. Abusers expect increasing compliance and obedience solely to their needs and wants, on the mistaken notion that perfect attunement and gratification and the release of all anger will result in the removal of internal pain and suffering, and a flooding of pleasure and serenity to compensate for the years of agony.

Rage becomes increasingly dominant over time. The body produces a maximum amount of hydrochloric acid and adrenaline in response to it. This causes a surge of energy, physiological stress, and readiness for action. There's a feeling of power and invulnerability, and an intense need to discharge the body's stress. Each rage incident lowers the threshold for future rage, so that, over time, formerly unimportant issues trigger the same or an even stronger response. This is not unlike a stimulant drug rush and the progression of addicts in chemical addictions.

The dynamics of people who abuse and are abused are similar in many ways. Both usually have domestic-violence role models from childhood, internalized negative self-images, a sense of inferiority, poor identity development and self-awareness, boundary problems, a high degree of fear and anxiety, an inability to address and resolve painful emotions and problems, poor communication skills, significant feelings of deprivation, severe distortions with dependency and responsibility, a fear of both abandonment and true intimacy, and a defensive, inappropriate over-focus on the partner to define personal satisfaction or dissatisfaction.

There are also parallels between a domestic-violence relationship and the relationship the addict has to the disease of addiction. Addicts commonly have a history of painful interactions with parents and/or others from their childhood environment, which they internalize to mean they are inferior, unlovable, unworthy and deserving only of continued mistreatment. Addicts commonly were habituated to danger, drama, chaos, and abuse in their families and learned to deny, rationalize, and minimize their feelings. Drugs additionally create a heightened level of defensiveness and an acceptance of antisocial behavior. This allows painful feelings and experiences to be denied, which, in turn, cuts off warning signals of current or impending danger.

Drugs, like the abuser in the early part of courtship, promise relief from pain and suffering and a flooding of bliss and peace. Drugs deceive, manipulate, and seduce potential addicts with a deadly ulterior motive. The disease doesn't trust anything outside itself or its own purposes. Addictive disease wants total attention from the addict and is possessive of the addict's thoughts, feelings, actions, and time. It wants to control, dominate, and enslave the addict as quickly as possible and is threatened by anyone or anything that wants to intervene in this control. The disease robs addicts of freedom, friendships, families, money, sanity, spirituality, positive self-esteem, a whole identity, and the ability to invest in and function effectively in life areas.

The disease doesn't take its own inventory or admit accountability for problems to the addict. Instead, it blames its consequences on people, places, and things. The disease traps the addict's mind in irrational, rigid thinking. The aim of the disease is to be all-powerful, so addicts can't see themselves as separate from their disease and have no life outside their drug experience. As the addict's dependence upon the drug increases, the drug's euphoria decreases in intensity and time, and dysphoria increases. Dysphoria causes more drug craving.

The disease wants the addict's need for drugs to increase while the pleasure of the drugs decreases and the damage done to the addict's life and the pain experienced escalates. The addict is mentally, emotionally, and physically abused by the drugs and yet feels unable to end the relationship, because the disease has killed off all awareness of strengths, resources, and tools to survive without drugs. The aim of the disease is sickness, suffering, pain, powerlessness, deprivation, and death. Whether for the untreated addict or the untreated partner in an abusive relationship, this is all too often the tragic ending.

....

Personal Growth Questions

1. In what ways do I relate to the addict or the abuser?
2. How did addiction or abuse escalate in my life and what prompted my desire for recovery?
3. Which dynamics from page 106 are relevant to me?

Affirmations

Today, I practice patience, tolerance, and understanding for myself and others.

I free myself from the bondage of false beliefs and embrace healing and happiness.

....

What's Our Motive?

If I give you something that I think you need or that I think is good for you, and you are not in agreement with me, then I am attempting to change you for my benefit. If I give you something that I like but you don't, I am trying to change your likes and dislikes to serve me. When I give you something you want in order to pressure you to give me something I want, I'm attempting to bribe you. When I give you something and remain attached to what you do with it or how you use it, I'm trying to manipulate you.

This does not mean that negotiating, requesting, evaluating, making deals with conditions, or trying to change someone is inappropriate. It is important, however, that we be clear about our motives and honest with others about what we are doing and why. It is inappropriate to believe that we are giving people something when we are merely attempting to control them for selfish purposes.

If I give you what you want because I want you to depend on me and not leave me, or because I'm living my life through you so I don't have to look at myself, or because I'm reinforcing my idea of you as selfish or incompetent and myself as a martyr or a success, or because I don't know how to set healthy limits and I need to blame you for this, I'm still controlling rather than giving.

In healthy adult relationships, we take responsibility for ourselves. We do not wait for others to take care of us, nor assume responsibility for others, nor coerce people to serve our needs. Part of personal responsibility is deciding with whom we are comfortable and with whom we are not comfortable in our lives and extending invitations and limits accordingly.

The depth of our self-awareness directly affects the quality of our relationships. When we lack personal insight regarding motives for our behaviors, we experience a far greater amount of anger, anxiety, confusion, and depression in relationships. And, unfortunately, we have no idea why this is.

To the extent that we believe we are responsible for other adults in our personal lives, or hold others responsible for us in adulthood, we deny our personal responsibility. This denial can manifest in outward problems or in symptoms that indicate the presence of significant emotional and mental pain and negativity. This framework guarantees unhappiness and failure in relationships.

Instead of focusing on the impact others have on us, we need to use those observations to initiate self-improvements. If we mistreat ourselves physically, mentally, emotionally, or spiritually, how can we be upset when others do so? If we fail to promote peace and harmony within, how can we complain of outer chaos and conflict? When we do not consistently support our own health and happiness, we must understand that we actively model for others how they should treat us. We reinforce habits that are less than desirable and shirk personal responsibility. Because these acknowledgements are unpleasant, we are likely to turn our focus back on others and thus repeat the negative cycle.

When we respond negatively to others' interactions, we can ask ourselves where this dynamic might exist in us. When we respond positively to others' interactions, we can take this as encouragement to further develop this trait in ourselves. When we focus attention on manipulating others for selfish needs, judging others, or fearing or expecting others to control us or take care of us, we attract a high degree of negative emotions.

We should also examine what we give to ourselves. Do we give ourselves excitement, or fear and worry? Do we give love, or condemnation, judgment, or hate? Are we impatient and perfectionist, or compassionate, encouraging, and understanding? Are we focusing on our defects and problems, or identifying and practicing the solutions to them? Do we keep ourselves small out of fear and insecurity, or are we supporting healthy steps forward to grow?

We bring more positive emotions into our lives by paying attention to and reinforcing self-caring attitudes and behaviors that increase positive esteem, spiritual growth, and health in all areas of life. Relationships with others will benefit from clear, honest, open communication, and sensitivity, respect, and mutual understanding. Either genuine acceptance, patience, and tolerance, or realistic boundaries, limits, and termination of relationships are important when conflicts continue unabated. When we've examined ourselves deeply and thoroughly, and our motives and behaviors have matured so that they are aligned with core spiritual values, all positive emotions are increased.

Personal Growth Questions

1. What are my examples of attempts to control others through giving?
2. How were or are my relationships affected by this?
3. How will my relationships evolve when I focus on only changing myself?

Affirmations

I deserve to transform old relationship patterns into healthier interactions.

As my personal responsibility increases, I attract more mature relationships.

Adult Children

Children living with an addicted or dysfunctional parent commonly feel that, if they can manage to please the parent sufficiently, the parent will then demonstrate love and nurturing and they will be happy. This can set in motion a pattern of codependent people-pleasing with ongoing frustration and confusion. Or the child may find areas in which to excel to make up for what was deficient in home life and become dependent on maintaining exhaustive and ever-increasing goals. Some children act out destructively to signal the pain inside themselves and their families, or develop false selves that are full of confidence and pseudo-maturity to deny the extent of dysfunction and consequent pain.

Addicted parents who are used to looking to drugs or other outside means to fix themselves, can also look to their children to fix them. Children internalize who they feel their parents need them to be, as well as their parents' identity. We develop mature interdependence from having a successful childhood dependency period and learning to give and receive reliable, healthy support. When our dependency is on a parent who's too ill to provide consistent nurturing, we can get stuck in dependency or premature independence. The latter is a defensive state. In order to be over-responsible in childhood, we have to defend against our needs to be taken care of, nurtured, and protected. Love and intimacy are then associated with inappropriate responsibilities for others, denial of personal feelings, and sacrificing true identity.

All of our adaptations to sick environments hide our real needs. Staunch independence hides our need to be vulnerable and receive reliable assistance. Manipulation and conning hides our need to be heard honestly and understood. Repression and denial hide our need to experience our feelings without judgment. Aggression hides our need to express pain and fear, and our need for empathetic responses. Competitiveness hides our need to know there is more than enough attention and support for us. Prostitution hides our need to have our bodies respected and valued without violation. Codependence hides our need to receive healthy caretaking experiences. Workaholism hides our need for unconditional love. These adaptations arise because it becomes too painful to acknowledge our real needs in an environment that is hostile or unresponsive to them.

Beliefs born of unhealthy family experiences can become self-fulfilling prophecies. I may be convinced that disaster is just around the corner, or that I'm unlovable, or that nothing I do is ever good enough, or that my opinions don't matter, or that it's selfish to think of my own feelings. Or perhaps I believe I'm better off dead. Our families may or may not have verbalized these feelings to us, but we internalize them from their example and their treatment of us. When we communicate and relate to others from painful past assumptions, we ensure continuing negative outcomes. We attract what is familiar and distort the unfamiliar to fit this blueprint. We do this because knowing what to expect and being prepared for it gives us the illusion that we're in control.

Life goals can also be rooted in childhood experience. We may pursue nursing from a frustrated need to fix a sick parent. We may go into a business that a parent values. Our goal may be to become wealthy because we grew up in an impoverished home. We may over-involve ourselves in our children's lives in response to an absence of involvement from our parents. We can marry someone with similar problems as a parent and try to please them, love them, or change them enough so that they are happy, thus making us happy. When our goals are not in sync with our natural talents and interests, but rather focus on healing or compensating for childhood pain, we will be gravely disappointed. We must directly address our personal problems, our family-of-origin problems, and the consequences from deficiencies and mistreatment in childhood.

Recovery affords us opportunities to return to our original needs and have corrective experiences. It allows us reality checks that challenge old belief systems, values, and behaviors. Once we have formed a healthy support system, we can practice letting go of defenses and begin to relate in an honest, open, and genuine manner. Identifying behaviors, thoughts, and feelings born of dysfunction, and realizing that we don't need them today, slowly disempowers them. Refusing to mistreat ourselves and others and setting firm, healthy boundaries for how we allow others to treat us is vital. Working through painful feelings from childhood heals the most powerful part of us. We need the child within us to be consciously re-parented. We need our adult recovery selves, with all our tools and support, to embrace, heal, and nurture the growth of this child. We are powerless to change the past, but recovery empowers us to change our present and therefore the future. Our adult lives can either repeat painful themes, or they can reflect the positive outcomes of healing.

Personal Growth Questions

1. How did I respond as a child to mistreatment or deficiencies from those who raised me?
2. What adaptations arose in me, and what healthy needs were repressed?
3. How do my childhood experiences affect my current significant others or family?

Affirmations

I commit to learning and practicing healthy re-parenting of my inner child.

I identify my true needs and successful means to fulfill them.

....

Solving Conflicts in Relationships

We make ourselves victims when we think others must change for us to be well. We are then dependent—much as children are dependent on their parents. In fact, this is the usual origin of relationship conflicts, especially with romantic partners. We unconsciously seek people who will trigger our unfinished business with our parents. Since we are powerless over other people, if we focus on their behaviors and attitudes toward us, and how and why they need to change, we will feel increasingly angry, anxious, frustrated, and forlorn.

The healthy alternative is to recognize that we attract partners with these specific issues because we need to heal in our responses to them. Discovering the parallel internal conflict and making that our focus empowers us and brings greater maturity to our relationships. For example, if I'm upset that my partner lacks emotional availability, I can ask myself what role emotional availability played in my family of origin and how it impacted me. Do I lack emotional bonding and quality attention to my own feelings? Do I expect constant emotional attunement and validation from my partner to compensate for its lack in my childhood? Do I consciously want my partner to be close emotionally and unconsciously feel I don't deserve this? If so, I'm sending mixed signals and am unable to receive and feel grateful for what is available to me.

If my partner's chronic anger bothers me, I can examine who was angry in my family of origin and how I responded to it. How do I express my anger? Do I judge anger as a "bad" feeling, or think it's the only way to be heard? If I only know passive or aggressive responses to anger, I need to learn assertiveness and how to set boundaries so that I am not victimized by another's unhealthy anger expression. If my anger is denied or repressed, it was buried alive and I will attract others to express it for me. If my partner and I are both chronically angry, I need to determine how I use anger as a defense to cover up more vulnerable feelings. I then need to heal the hurt, pain, and fear below the anger.

If I feel belittled by my partner's constant criticism of me, I can question whether I also judge myself or others harshly. Do I suffer from feelings of inferiority and, if so, when did these feelings first begin? Have I developed my identity so that my view of myself has a balance of strengths and weaknesses? Have I denied my parents' criticism of me and shifted blame for all of my early problems onto my current partner? Are my expectations and standards for myself and others too high or too low?

I am not suggesting that we remain in unsafe relationships while we analyze ourselves. Nor am I suggesting that we not express to our partners how we feel in response to them or make requests that they change. Communication with our partners, about both positive and negative elements of the relationship, is a vital part of healthy intimacy, especially when stated non-defensively and non-offensively. Responsibility for the solution of our painful feelings in the relationship belongs to us, however. Recovery is a personal commitment to take healthy care of ourselves, to know what is acceptable and what is not acceptable to us, and to let go of what is harmful, to actively address character defects and apply spiritual principles in all of our affairs.

We attract partners on our level of emotional maturity, which means that problems in relationships signal work we deserve to do inside of ourselves. Personal and family-of-origin inventories are critical to turning problems into opportunities for learning and growth. When we change significantly, our partners will change.

This does not mean that our partners will necessarily change to our benefit, however. Sometimes, our highest healthy interests are not served by a particular relationship.

Communicating concerns over problems, realizing similarities between new and old problems, identifying and changing our part in these problems so that we are in sync with our spiritual beliefs is our responsibility. Observing what direction the relationship takes when we've done our work, will determine whether or not the relationship is in our best interest. Living in integrity means that our daily lives reflect our highest principles in thought, emotion, and action. As adults, we do not need others to change so that we can be well. In partnership with our Higher Power, we are responsible for our well-being and continued growth, and that determines the quality of all other relationships.

....

Personal Growth Questions

1. In what ways does my partner mirror aspects of myself or members of my family of origin?
2. What are my negative responses to conflicts? What positive responses could replace them?
3. What do I need to heal and learn in order to improve relationships?

I accept responsibility for my part
in relationship problems and I choose
positive change in these areas now.

I am willing to release what fails to serve,
and to embrace what supports my
healthy relationship goals.

....

Intimate Recovery

We unite with each other because we have lessons to learn that only the trials and joys of intimacy can reveal. The model for relationships originates from our childhood experience of our parents' relationship and their interaction with us. Positive experiences in marriage are usually similar to positive experiences in our families of origin, or are wished-for compensations for what we felt deprived of in childhood. Negative experiences in marriage generally reflect similar themes, feelings, and dynamics from our families of origin. We are unconsciously attracted to mates who trigger familiar feelings of positive, negative, and wish elements from early life. Examining our reactions to our spouses allows us to determine what needs healing inside of us. Our task is to identify and ultimately transform what blocks us from fully giving and receiving love, so that we mature beyond the limits of early modeling.

All too often, however, we expect our spouses to repair the damage done to us by imperfect parents. As long as we have not fully healed from childhood wounds, we will attract partners who seem to, or do, hurt us in similar ways. The program tells us to communicate and act from spiritual principles, regardless of whether the other person does so. The most difficult person with whom to practice this is an intimate partner, yet this is where the most healing and growth are needed.

We internalize health from the healthy parts and sickness from the sick parts of our families while growing up. We use defense mechanisms to cope with unhealthy aspects of life. Over time, these coping strategies become an intrinsic part of our identities, so that our expectations and participation in dysfunction is automatic and unquestioned. Honest, deep, and thorough inventories are necessary in order to identify unconscious patterns that prevent growth. In the early stages of surrendering old thinking and behaviors, we often feel overly exposed and vulnerable. For some of us, it's a kind of death, because so much of our identity stems from defenses.

Focusing on our own beliefs and behaviors rather than those of our partners sustains recovery. Expecting our mates to change elements reminiscent of our own past problems increases conflict, tension, and defensiveness. It also fails to address the root of the problem, which is within us. Instead of complaining, for instance, that our spouses don't support us sufficiently, the more important question is who failed us similarly in child-hood and in what ways are we not supporting ourselves currently. Rather than focusing on our mates' dependency, we can explore premature or excessive responsibilities that were given to us in early life, ways in which we are dependent, or how we need someone to depend on us to feel valued. If our partners are abusive, until we are prepared to leave the relationship without attracting another abusive relationship, we must ask what conditions in our families of origin fostered abuse and victimization and what in our self-image and behaviors reinforces the same.

When we change our response to elements that triggered pain and defenses in the past, conflict decreases. When we meet our healthy needs and heal the effects of original pain, our hearts open to a higher level of love. When we practice honesty and humility, we cease attempts to control. When we refrain from harm and intrusion, we invite harmony and peace. When we practice patience, tolerance, compassion, and understanding, we surrender false beliefs and gain wisdom. When we value vulnerability as much as potency, closeness as much as separateness, we experience a balance of individual and relationship growth. When we ask for divine will to be done in our relationships, we ask for our highest goals to be achieved. When we give all we have to give, despite the possibility of loss, our love is genuine.

The most important question we need to answer is how our relationships reflect our spiritual strengths and weaknesses. We can always improve, because the evolution of love never ends. There's a place deep inside of us where all needs are met, where love is unconditional, complete, and eternal. It is the place where we are united with the God of our understanding. Our goal is to find and experience this place in ourselves, our partners, and in life, as frequently and as fully as we can.

....

Personal Growth Questions

1. Which positive, negative, and wish elements from my family of origin are present in my current relationships?
2. What negative and positive behaviors from my family of origin are present in my current relationships?
3. What are the roots of my present conflicts and how can I demonstrate positive change in these areas?

Affirmations

Examining my part in relationship difficulties allows me to transform key weaknesses into strengths.

I am capable of giving and receiving the highest levels of love.

....

Take Time to Nurture Yourself

Nurturing ourselves means discovering what internal and external conditions ideally suit us and consistently providing these elements for ourselves. After years of self-destructive beliefs and behaviors, nurturing does not come easily. We must spend quality time with ourselves to develop a deeper awareness and emotional attunement. We can do this through journaling, meditation, visual imagery, daydreaming, self-reflection and analysis, exploring and processing feelings, and by sharing and receiving feedback from people whom we trust to understand us and this process.

There are important questions we can ask to determine our specific nurturing needs. In what environments do we thrive? How do we protect ourselves from harm? What are our most important needs and wants? What are our personal strengths and weaknesses? What do we value most? What personality traits do we like and dislike in ourselves? What talents and gifts do we have? What absorbs our attention completely? What do we fear? What do we wish to surrender? Where do we want to put down roots? What do we enjoy? What relaxes us? How much time and space do we need just for ourselves on a daily basis? Who enriches us and challenges our growth? Who invades our space and takes from us? What are our personal growth goals and what must we release, acquire, and develop to accomplish them?

All of us have relationships with ourselves and often, when we haven't consciously evaluated and developed these relationships, they are based on unhealthy past influences and experiences. We may have learned to avoid our feelings or needs, or to abuse ourselves verbally or impose perfectionist standards on what we do. If we were not nurtured in childhood, we can explore the caring we wished we had received. Children typically need healthy food, safety, warmth, a home without undue stress, affection, attention, a feeling of belonging and being valued, reliability, emotional attunement and validation, understanding, a model for coping with difficult feelings and problems, joy, laughter, play, serenity, and love. When caretakers consistently provide these elements, we internalize them and they become our foundation for lifelong self-nurturing. When they haven't been provided, we need to develop them in ourselves using healthy role models to assist us.

Paying more attention to our inner dialogue and how we talk to, feel toward, and treat ourselves can illuminate how deprived or fulfilled our nurturing needs were in childhood. Many of us are comforting and compassionate with others and hostile, unforgiving, and demanding with ourselves. We need to start speaking to ourselves with unconditional love. This will then allow us to feel safe and secure in a deeper exploration of our thoughts and feelings. Even when we experience pain or recognize unhealthy behavior in ourselves, we must respond with full attention and honesty. When we confront ourselves, we can do so firmly and compassionately. Our need is to understand ourselves better—mentally, emotionally, and physically—so that we can heal, learn, and grow. This enables us to acquire inner strength, resiliency, greater appreciation, and sensitivity.

We can pay attention to experiences that remind us of past pain and process our feelings to increase understanding and healing. We can learn from our bodies what prompts relaxation and tension responses and what increases and decreases our energy. When our bodies tense, we can identify internal or external causes and change either the situation or our response to it. Balancing what we give to others and what we give to ourselves stops us from feeling depleted. The more we tune in to ourselves, the more we can distinguish the healthy parts of us from the parts we internalized from sick environments. Then we can disempower the latter. As we practice internal bonding, we increasingly trust our feelings and instincts to lead us to healthy solutions and fulfillment.

Self-nurturing is physical, mental, and emotional. All that we do to promote health and to heal and protect ourselves from further sickness is of the utmost importance. Inner nourishment includes eating healthy food, exercise, setting aside time for undivided attention to our inner lives, play, relaxation, hobbies, enrichment experiences, pampering, creative work, and following through with personal growth goals. It includes spending time with people who are positive influences for us and fully accepting the healthy love that exists in our lives today. Self-nurturing allows us to discover our inner wounds and inner wealth, and our purpose and plan to actualize our unique potential in life.

....

Personal Growth Questions

1. What are the negative and positive elements of my relationship with myself?
2. How do I answer some of the questions in paragraph two?
3. What physical sensations arise when I have negative and positive experiences?

Affirmations

I increasingly create conditions for positive feelings and experiences so that they are a familiar, fundamental part of my life.

I nurture my mental, emotional, and physical well-being on a daily basis.

....

Answers to Prayers

When we ask for divine assistance, we sometimes find out how attached we are to our character defects, defense mechanisms, and willfulness. These are the things that prevent us from reaching our recovery goals. It is our responsibility to examine our problems, including obstacles to achieving our goals, to determine how we acquired them and what internal dynamics maintain them. If our habitual behaviors and thoughts fail to bring us sufficient happiness and health, no amount of external gratification or change can compensate for this. When we repeatedly request, in prayer, a solution for the consequences of what we have sown and reaped, we ask God to rescue us from our unwillingness to examine ourselves, learn, and mature. Demonstrating personal responsibility allows us to build competence, confidence, and positive esteem. For God to do for us what we can do for ourselves, without prompting our learning and growth, would be codependent.

To receive something new, we must surrender something old. This is not because the Almighty requires a sacrifice from us, but because we are complete creations, lacking nothing for our own lives' purpose. Therefore, our problem is that we've allowed artificial barriers to hide what we now seek. Defenses prevent our conscious awareness and experience of all that is within us. When we pray for greater patience, for example, we may then have a series of experiences in which we become excessively impatient. Likewise, praying to feel more loving may bring interactions that activate anger, jealousy, and lust. Examining the triggers for these reactions allows us to explore where, when, and under what circumstances these kinds of responses first occurred.

We often find that our issues began in childhood with our families of origin. As dependent children, we cannot control many things, and people and experiences have a much more powerful and lasting effect on us. As adults, this is less so. God's answers to these prayers can thus motivate us to look closely at the specific impediments to our goals, and lead us to seek to understand their genesis and begin a process of surrendering them.

Reactions that are significantly stronger than what the circumstances typically elicit indicate that they are based in old experiences where we lacked maturity, resourcefulness, independence, and knowledge. In addition, our values, priorities, and beliefs change with increasing exposure to education, and our own and others' experiences. Old habits, however, can have a stronger influence on us than newer ideas, especially when situations remind us of the past. The solution is to remind ourselves regularly what is true for us now in our adulthood, recognize the differences between past and present situations that stimulate a similar response, and finally to stop old impulses from finding full expression and replace them with what is appropriate for us today.

Accepting responsibility to change ourselves in a positive direction invites divine assistance. God gives us guidance and tools commensurate with our abilities to use them. Sometimes, we don't like them; sometimes, we simply don't use them; sometimes, we believe our prayers have not been answered, because we're expecting a specific answer of our ego's choosing. Sometimes, we pray according to others' views, and are afraid that an answer will require more from us than what we are willing to give. At other times, we think we're prepared to receive God's help in some area and God knows that we are not. God responds to our energy and feelings and, when the words of our prayers are not aligned with our deeper truth, the answer responds to that deeper truth.

Prayers can also be answered in ways that are recognizable and immediately gratifying. This occurs when our human needs and wants are compatible with either our soul's purpose or the soul purpose of others for whom we are praying. When our actions, feelings, and thoughts are of a positive nature and work cohesively to prepare us to receive what we desire, we are likely to receive just that. Answers to prayers can come in the form of insight, feelings, or internal or external change, depending on what will bring us the most learning and growth. Setting aside time on a daily basis for meditation or quiet relaxation allows us a greater opportunity to receive conscious responses to our prayers. Regular meditation also makes it more likely that we will experience a harmonious interplay of our human and spiritual aspects and a higher understanding of God's role in our lives.

Personal Growth Questions

1. Discuss a prayer experience where you refused to accept appropriate personal responsibility.
2. Discuss a prayer experience that allowed you to acquire insight and growth.
3. Discuss a prayer experience that was immediately gratifying.

Affirmations

I am willing to learn about my soul's purpose
by examining my prayers and their answers.

I am grateful for God's guidance in helping
me to understand my higher truth.

....

Chapter 4

The Process of Growth
and Transformation

IT IS NATURAL FOR US, AS HUMANS, to pursue pleasure and attempt to prevent pain. Ideally, role models demonstrate healthy means to meet important wants and needs, and to address pain in ways that minimize damage and encourage understanding and growth. When we lack healthy examples, we are open to what will bring short-term relief and give us the illusion or seeming potential of rewards.

The Process of Addiction and Treatment

Drugs initially offer rushes of pleasure, feelings of peace, a numbing of pain, surges of power and energy, positive self and life feelings, diminishing pressure and stress, and altered reality. In the early stages of use, this is a panacea, especially for someone with a background of trauma. As use becomes abuse and then addiction, the panacea becomes a nightmare. By this time, however, drugs have damaged and altered the chemistry and function of the brain. The primitive part of the brain, which controls habits, basic emotions, and reward and pleasure, is reinforced. The more evolved part of the brain fails to function normally. This leads to the irrational thinking and insane behavior of addiction. Drugs are pursued over everyone and everything at any cost because of the drugs' effects on the brain.

In addition to drugs, defenses aid in blocking awareness of painful truths. Defenses take energy from us and reinforce our sense of powerlessness over our problems and pain. Defenses create new symptoms and problems and prevent us from insight, resolution, and growth. Just like drugs, we acquire tolerance to defenses—which, in order to work, must escalate.

As addiction progresses, the promise of euphoria is replaced with its polar opposite. Instead of pleasure, there is paranoia and panic. In place of peace, there is violence. Pain, pressure, and stress intensify. Negative feelings about self and life are inescapable. Altered reality is now a nightmare that often ends in death. Addiction takes away jobs, finances, freedom, health, loved ones, safety, self-respect, sanity, and lives on an epidemic basis. Addiction gives guilt, shame, rage, horror, helplessness, depression, fear, phobias, and failure free reign. This is how addictive disease betrays its promise of paradise.

Incarceration typically reinforces defenses and deviant behaviors. Addicts report that the associations between their painful past experiences both prior to and during drug use are triggered in our jail and prison systems. Without skills to address these issues in healthy ways, the disease of addiction gains more strength, even with periods of abstinence.

In order for addicts to make positive use of treatment, the environment must be safe and provide ample resources for psychological and physiological healing. The purpose of treatment is to help addicts transfer their dependency on drugs to a dependency on a healthy, helpful Higher Power. Treatment staff must model unity, spirituality, fellowship, and maturity. Staff should assist addicts in distinguishing between the healthy and sick parts of their minds and provide successful intervention strategies. In addition, recovering addicts must conduct a rigorously honest and deep self and life appraisal. This enables them to identify and take steps to surrender all sick thinking and behaviors.

Not only do we need to understand the harm addiction causes, we need to establish healthy sources of pleasure, peace, positive energy, and feelings, as well as appropriate responses to address and heal pain and resolve problems. Beliefs, values, priorities, styles of communication, and emotional processing, as well as relationship dynamics must be developed that support recovery. These new healthy patterns must then be practiced and reinforced in the recovery environment. Because there is no cure for addictive disease, and because we are creatures of habit and vulnerable to return to what is most familiar, it is imperative that ongoing support for recovery be the highest priority for addicts completing treatment.

Addiction and defenses keep us from our inner truths. We're afraid to look inside, thinking it will overwhelm us with helplessness and hopelessness. And yet it is only when we examine truth in its entirety that we can understand what our real solutions are. Helplessness and hopelessness happen when we put drugs and defenses in charge of ourselves and our lives. Now it is our responsibility to put our healthy Higher Power and our program of recovery in control. If we believe in a loving God, then we know we are not meant to suffer or administer impoverishment or abuse. We don't need illusions of peace or power, and we are not dependent upon people, places, and things for our happiness. When we stop pursuing an artificial pretense of paradise, and embrace the spiritual principles of our program, we find a more fulfilling and rewarding life than we ever dreamed possible.

Personal Growth Questions

1. What are the ways in which I have pursued pleasure and dulled pain? What have been the consequences?
2. Who in my life inspires, motivates, and guides me to healthier means of happiness and resolution of pain?
3. What do I do that allows me to experience a natural sense of serenity?

Affirmations

I choose to cause no further pain to myself or others, and to promote peace and well-being to the best of my ability.

I follow suggestions from healthy people I admire today and choose life experiences that help me feel closer to my Higher Power.

....

Where Are We Going?

As children, we wish to be loved, nurtured, valued, and understood. We need our caretakers to set healthy boundaries and teach us limits so that we are safe, secure, and able to get along with others. We are unique individuals with natural talents and interests that excite and motivate us to live creatively, proactively, and assertively. When we experience painful emotions and people in our lives help us understand rather than judge us, we learn resiliency and the power of inner healing and strength. When we have healthy models for love, support, and understanding, we internalize a healthy love for ourselves and are able to enjoy mutually fulfilling relationships.

Contrast this with those who grow up with addiction or other significant illness, cruelty, incest, violence, abandonment, neglect, chronic confusion, or chaos. If we live in a sick environment, especially as children, we adapt to it in order to survive. These adaptations lead to a host of unhealthy attitudes and behaviors. If the people in our lives are unable to care for us in important ways, we get stuck in a reactive place where we aggressively or passively respond to our environment rather than assertively develop from who we are. We erect massive defenses against our real selves because they carry too much pain and are being rejected by our environment. This creates a pervasive sense of emptiness that no amount of external riches or compulsions can fix. Nevertheless, this is typically where we end up, desperately trying to fool ourselves that satisfying compulsions will lead us to fulfillment, despite overwhelming evidence to the contrary as addiction progresses. Addictions and compulsions can't work, because the real problem or need isn't being addressed. We can't let go of pain until we understand it. We can't find real joy and love until we stop running from ourselves.

Our common response to personal damage and deprivation is to close our hearts, constrict our thinking to defensive or offensive approaches, and act from isolated fragments rather than from the whole of ourselves. This kind of response deepens our attachment to damage and deprivation. We over-personalize pain, to the point of accepting our responses to it as our identities and as our lives. We become possessive of our specific pain and reinforce its reality by focusing on similarities between current and past experiences. Thus we ensure that our lives remain the same.

We fail to see how our compulsions do not serve our health and happiness, and we disregard new experiences that could expand our learning, our identities, and our lives. Addictions and compulsions are manifestations of arrested thought patterns surrounded by defenses. Where they exist, there is no creativity, curiosity, exploration, or growth. And because defenses protect our full awareness of problems, we don't realize our active participation in reaffirming what works against us. Once thought patterns are repeated to the point of habituation, they are automatically sustained. If they originated from false or limited beliefs, we will perpetuate life routines that prevent maturation. It is newness, not sameness, which allows us to grow.

Typically, the only thing that disrupts the process of addiction is when the compulsion itself finally fails to satisfy internal needs. When the pain and negative consequences of addiction are more powerful than its euphoria, and the hope of finding fulfillment of important needs is stronger than the fear of further pain and rejection, we are receptive to recovery. Despite diminishing returns from the compulsion, the power we've given it in the past to override conflicting actions, thoughts, and feelings fights these new efforts to surrender it. We need assistance and we attach ourselves with fervor to the fellowship that befriends us. We write long lists of ways addiction caused us pain. We listen and follow direction in order to feel safe and sound. We change our actions, re-examine beliefs, and let go of all forms of harming in order to amend our lives. This is how we empower our whole selves in a healthy way, and grow beyond our addiction.

Just as we wished others had done with us in childhood, we learn to pay attention with deep sustained interest to the whole of our experience. We maintain compassion for ourselves while confronting and terminating destructive attitudes and behaviors. We face our fears and walk through pain with open hearts, knowing that we are not alone. We create safe environments and healthy boundaries, so that we enjoy ourselves and others. We remain teachable and interested in fulfilling our highest positive potential.

....

Personal Growth Questions

1. What was my most difficult conflict or pain in childhood?
2. How has this been recreated in my adult life and what are my adult responses?
3. How can I change my part in these experiences so that I act and communicate in a more mature manner?

Affirmations

I pay attention to my assumptions,
attitudes, and behaviors, and identify
whether they originate from past pain
or from current recovery principles.

I willingly change my behaviors and thoughts
to support positive personal growth.

....

Fake, Fate, or Faith?

When we chase after people, places, and things to make us happy, we have failed to grasp who we truly are. Our Higher Power becomes the next conquest or acquisition. We invest in a fake self, because we believe the real one won't get us what we want. We are dependent upon others' approval, because we have none that's genuine for ourselves. We're either aggressive or passive-aggressive, because assertiveness requires responsibility for the selves we avoid. Our words and actions spring solely from selfish motives. We betray others as we have betrayed ourselves. We use self-righteousness and perpetual activity to deflect the gnawing anxiety in our guts. When we fail to begin with truth, we disable integrity and forfeit happiness and harmony. All we're left with is an egomaniacal shell.

Fate generally takes a more passive approach. We're victims resigned to a fragmented focus and a deficiency of energy. We have the universe within and without to explore, yet our fears hold us hostage to repeating a small slice of life. We deny our nature to evolve and create. We fail to support ourselves with any consistency and will sabotage success if it comes too close. We are full of fear and we project it onto life itself. We are angry, for we have made ourselves impotent. We have no peace and can find nothing of substance to give or receive. We stand astride a precipice, with one foot in desire and one foot in helplessness. We can't release either one without falling.

Faith is a working partnership that engages and enlarges our awareness of self, life, and our true potential. To awaken spiritually means that we experience profound positive changes in thoughts, feelings, and actions. Since dishonesty and defensiveness enable addictions and dysfunctions to develop and progress, our recovery is directly dependent upon how honest, deep, and thorough our personal inventory is. We examine ourselves specifically to understand how our identity and life-style evolved, and to determine what promotes and what impedes spiritual growth.

Addictions and compulsions are characterized by impulsiveness, willfulness, and inability to defer gratification. These traits generally develop in reaction to chronic feelings of abandonment or deprivation, abuse or over-control, and a lack of compassion or understanding. Therefore, in order to surrender them, our recovery support must be readily available, have healthy role models, be able to assist and teach us positive ways to meet our needs, treat us with respect and sensitivity, accept that it is our right to continue or discontinue recovery, and demonstrate empathy and understanding of our feelings, thoughts, and experiences.

Self-examination and discussion with others in recovery help us to see how easy it is for us to internalize and practice harmful behaviors that we endured, especially in childhood. The process of healing, learning, and maturing in recovery allows us ultimately to forgive ourselves and others, and lessens our tendency toward judgment, hatred, and prejudice. Additionally, re-experiencing pain with greater understanding gives us compassion for all suffering and decreases our inclination to harm in the future. Understanding how deeply rooted our unhealthy behavior is, and how much time and effort is required for profound positive change, helps us to develop patience, tolerance, and humility.

Recognizing the extent and pervasiveness of human suffering enables us to surrender self-pity, arrogance, and grandiosity. We find ourselves drawn to helping others as we have been and continue to be helped. Being of service reinforces our personal commitment to positive change, allows harmonious relationships to develop, and urges us to be accountable to daily living that reflects our feelings and current beliefs and values.

We have free will to turn against our spiritual nature and invest in mundane materialism and earthly values. Problems and pain can be perceived as evidence of a punishing or nonexistent God. We may believe life is a game of alternating defensive and offensive positions, and that winning and losing is predicated solely upon

Grace Lost and Found

the ego's sense of power and pride. When our energy and focus attends only to the world we see with our five senses, it can be difficult to find higher purpose and meaning. The more painful our life experiences, the more important healing is to ultimately transforming confusion and anguish into learning and growth. The more captivated we are by possessions, the less we are able to see the mighty magnificence of our souls—or even of a giant redwood tree, for that matter. It is only when we decide to take that magical leap of faith and entwine our will with divine will that higher purpose can be revealed and our true potential achieved.

....

Personal Growth Questions

1. What is an example of my faking who I am?
2. What is an example of my acting, feeling, or thinking like a victim in adulthood?
3. What effects do faking or feeling like a victim have on me today?

Affirmations

I ask that divine will work through me for my highest good.

I allow my character defects to transform into character assets.

....

The Spirituality of Recovery

If we believe that the God of our understanding creates life, then we realize our divine origin. Human beings have free will, however, which allows for substantial deviations from spiritual practices. We enter this world open to experience and desirous of conditions that will enable us to thrive. Any elements discordant with our best interests are experienced as pain. The more pain we experience without resolution, the more we mistrust and withdraw from inner and outer awareness. When our healthy needs are denied, we learn to settle for much less than what we deserve. Defenses become our means for survival when we have no other models or tools. Like scars covering wounds, they enable us to function in dysfunction. Yearning still exists, however, for a far better experience of self and life. For some, this leads to drug use and can progress to addiction.

Addictive disease is not just putting drugs, which are poisons, into our bodies. It's embracing abuse, crime, defense mechanisms, dishonesty, irresponsibility, insane thinking and behavior, paranoia, prostitution, self-loathing, shame, and violence. Anything good in our lives at this time is either lost or becomes sick, because we are lost and sick. Every wound given and received that goes unhealed and unenlightened is poisonous to us and others. We're a toxic waste dump of sick actions, attitudes, beliefs, feelings, goals, and values, and we threaten everyone and everything in our paths. Our lives lack purpose, substance, and spirituality. We accept poor imitations of needs and delude ourselves into thinking this is what we really want.

We settle for sex because we can't recall what love is. We settle for the street because we've lost directions to the homes inside of our souls. We settle for control because we have nothing of value to share or receive. We settle for violence because we have no inner strength. We settle for incarceration because we've so severely narrowed and denigrated the possibilities for our lives. We settle for self-righteousness because we're afraid of the depth and mystery of God. We settle for drug highs because we've forgotten our heavenly heritage.

The disease of addiction tells us that all we need is a never-ending supply of drugs and we will feel ecstatic, loved, powerful, safe, satisfied, and serene. We often do feel these things during the honeymoon period of drug use. As addiction progresses, the physiological dependence becomes more powerful than the psychological dependence, making it difficult to stop using, even if we realize the desired effects have dwindled. When we're ashamed, beaten, broken, dirty, disgusted, scared, and sick enough to ask for help, however, we begin to see more clearly just how far into madness and deceit we've descended.

Recovery tells us that we can no longer afford to run from pain and hide from truth. We must examine ourselves and our lives thoroughly and deeply, disman tle every one of our false beliefs, experience our emotions without defenses, and change our actions to reflect the principles of recovery. We must find the God of our understanding and cultivate that relationship before all others. The foundation for recovery is continuous spiritual fitness. We need to remember that we are children of God, and let our lives demonstrate this truth. If we believe that God is the source of the highest form of love, and life is created from that love, then our task is to identify and develop everything good within us and give those gifts freely to others.

With God as our teacher and parent, we can interrupt the flood of fears and experience the silence that brings peace to our souls. We can love ourselves rather than force conditions on our worth. We can recognize that life is a gift and that each day is sacred, rather than rush through time distracted and inattentive. When we know that God's love has no beginning or end, we can believe in eternity. When we forget that, we fear change and death. When we accept that no problem is too small or too large for God, we have faith that our problems will ultimately be transformed into lessons, growth, and new ways to help others.

God knows that we become wounded, scarred, and armored in life. God knows that the armor becomes a dagger that re-wounds. God asks us to remember that we were given the gift of free will and that we are here to grow. To learn the secret of healing, we must be wounded and wound. To learn maturity, we must lose, and then regain our spiritual wisdom. To learn the way back to paradise, we must become all that God intended for us. There are thousands of ways to be sick and there is one way to become well. That way is to surrender our free will back to God. When we say "Thy will be done on earth as it is in Heaven," that is how we discover the kingdom of Heaven within us. That is how we stay connected to the unending source of God's goodness and how recovery blesses us divinely.

....

Personal Growth Questions

1. What were the worst consequences of my unbridled willfulness?
2. What are some of my gifts and how do I use them?
3. Discuss a problem that transformed into learning and growth.

Affirmations

I will identify and ask God
to help me surrender my negative energy
as I become aware of it.

I will acknowledge and value
my positive gifts, and share them
with others who are receptive to them.

....

Inside Recovery

If we were irresponsible practicing our addiction, sometimes we compensate for this by being overly responsible today. Once we progress through the primary steps of recovery, we find there's a natural high from behaving appropriately and responsibly. Others see us as trustworthy and reliable; we are accomplishing more than we ever thought possible, and we like ourselves this way. External productivity is a positive outcome of recovery, but this can become a new compulsion. Unless we balance outer with inner productivity, we can end up chasing the high of the completed list, needing the adrenaline rush of constant activity, and worrying that doing it all won't be enough.

What newcomers need in recovery is the warm extension of welcome, heartfelt understanding, patient listening, and borrowed faith from others that pain does pass. We don't outgrow these needs, but we can internalize healthy caretaking so that we can do this for ourselves, and for others when appropriate. Redirecting dependency on drugs to dependency on treatment and program allows us to identify and begin to meet our primary healthy needs. Treatment fosters the growth and development of skills to address and resolve pain and problems.

Conversely, addictions and compulsions feed defenses and pitiful illusions of peace, power, and happiness. Our real selves are recklessly abandoned in favor of falsehoods. In order to block awareness of pain, we must block our identities and all feelings and thoughts that trigger vulnerability, including our ability to give and receive love. This is one reason why addiction breeds a deep sense of aloneness, even when the addict is surrounded by people. When the truth holds unbearable pain, altering our perceptions may seem like the only option. As addiction progresses, we return to our

Grace Lost and Found

original pain with less ability and strength to cope than ever. And we have the additional burden of pain and problems from addiction.

Recovery happens when we are honest, open-minded, and willing to face what we don't know. We are far more than the sum of our thoughts, feelings, and actions. We are all connected to something deeper. When we obsessively and compulsively order our lives, it clouds the core of connection to something greater than ourselves. Assuming more control than is realistic, possible, or necessary is the hallmark of avoiding inner chaos. Being compulsively busy hides emptiness and loss. And acting like a super-responsible adult covers previously unmet dependency needs.

We can practice being visible to ourselves and observe our thoughts, feelings, and actions. We learn to differentiate between needs and wants that serve recovery and growth, and those that come from addiction and unhealthy role models. Complacency or compulsivity do not serve us. We must allow recovery to challenge and change us continually, and attend to our inner responses. When we cry over a movie, something important in us wants attention. When a song stirs our souls, we need to stop what we're doing and experience the depth of those feelings. When we notice something extraordinary in an ordinary moment, we enlarge our view of life. Sometimes we drift so far from our inner needs that it takes physical pain to make us listen.

If the progress we make in our external lives is to be balanced with internal growth, we must reclaim or discover our true identities, practice being vulnerable in situations where it's safe to do so, and learn how to give and receive healthy love. We are the only ones who are present to ourselves from birth to death. No one else has our specific interests, talents, personality, and life purpose. No one but we ourselves can walk our paths. Our inside lives are the foundation and our outer lives are the manifestation of our relationships with ourselves and our Higher Power. When our actions in the world are dictated by a taskmaster of responsibility in our minds, we move backward. When what we value most is at the heart of how we work in the world, our paths naturally evolve to fulfillment.

....

Personal Growth Questions
1. Of what external accomplishments am I most proud?
2. What internal changes have I made that support genuine positive self-esteem?
3. In what areas of my life am I complacent? In what areas am I compulsive? What am I hiding as a result of this?

Affirmations
I will dedicate time to quiet inner reflection and healing on a regular basis.

I will include time in my daily schedule for the things I most value.

....

Grace Lost and Found

How Strong Is Our Recovery?

When we pretend to be other than who we are to win acceptance, we abandon ourselves. When we criticize another in an attempt to glorify ourselves, we are demeaned. When we profess love based on idealization or denial, we delude ourselves. When we forgive someone for harm done to us, yet haven't examined, understood, or healed from the harm, we reinforce our fears. When we punish our children for behaviors and attitudes that we currently practice, we are hypocrites. When we help others so that we can avoid facing our own problems, we are codependent. When we give to others in order to control them, we are dishonest and devious. These are all examples of failures to practice faith in the recovery process. We are avoiding the very vulnerability that we need in order to heal and grow.

Our motives and underlying belief systems need to be examined to determine whether our behaviors and attitudes are recovery-based. Outwardly, we may look like a positive example of a program. Inwardly, whenever we shy away from deep, fearless inventory, we suffer spiritually and psychologically. Pretense and half truths are an important part of the problem for which we sought help. They have no place in the solution.

Addiction brings bondage to a sick substitute for acceptance and pleasure. True self esteem and joy are the benefits of a process of rigorous inventory and personal transformation. Every addiction has an intricate, interwoven support system that consists of character defects, unhealthy attitudes and actions, false beliefs, defenses, fears, and often hatred of internal and external realities. Its effect on every area of life must be examined and healthy alternatives identified and practiced. Breaking the cycle of addiction is easier than dismantling the support system for it. Its support, however, is the genesis of misery, compulsions, failure, and relapse.

Identifying and surrendering all that hampers recovery cannot be accomplished without help. Unconscious defense mechanisms and lack of awareness and understanding prevent us from clear, deep reflection. The perceptions of sponsors, peers in recovery, and counselors can enlarge and enlighten our view. Once sick and unproductive thinking and behaviors are identified, their surrender requires assistance from our Higher Power. Daily prayer, attention and correction when we falter, and learning and practicing substitute thoughts and actions are necessary.

If negativity or abuse helped us to heal, learn, and grow, we would have no addictions. The purpose of the program's inventory is to understand ourselves and identify the areas where solutions are needed. Pain and hope are key components of motivation for change. Pain, in this case, is not masochistic, but rather the acknowledgement of pain we and others experience as a result of untreated addictions and dysfunction. Sickness produces suffering for us and others. Programs advise us to pray for people who are sick, rather than express anger or despair toward them. We must apply this equally to ourselves. Compassion, honesty, and understanding create a safe space for hope and faith to flourish.

We must form new connections between ourselves and others. Mature caring evolves from understanding. Understanding comes from slowing down, deep breathing, prayer, meditation, self-reflection, and listening for deeper answers. Underneath every unhealthy behavior is a false belief. Underneath every false belief is pain in need of healing. When we heal and let go of what no longer works for us, we experience rejuvenation. There is room for us to grow and an openness to new ideas.

Life on life's terms means that we accept negative and positive, loss and gain, sickness and health, stress and serenity. Life is change. Resisting change causes us to live in fear and darkness. When we respond to conflict, stress, and wounding with aggression, despair, or denial we are in opposition to life. When our response is to challenge ourselves to grow to greater maturity, we are collaborating with life.

All the energy that we send out into the world returns to us magnified. Thoughts, feelings, actions, and their underlying motives work either for or against us. The strength of our commitment to recovery determines the amount of struggle and harmony we will experience. We are all given a unique combination of talents by a power greater than ourselves. When we waste or exploit them in harmful ways, we turn talents into enemies. When we identify, nurture, and express them for the highest good, we become the blessing we are meant to be.

Personal Growth Questions

1. What actions, attitudes, and beliefs hinder my recovery? How do these things affect me emotionally, mentally, physically, and spiritually?

2. What healthy actions, attitudes, and beliefs can replace the ones contrary to recovery?

3. What is one internal and one external goal and my motivational factors for their achievement? Do I believe they are aligned with my Higher Power's will for me?

Affirmations

I will examine my underlying motives for actions and decisions, and follow through with those that are in sync with divine will.

I understand that my greatest health and happiness arise when I place my spiritual growth above short-term gratification.

....

Drugs of Choice and Their Corollaries

Symptoms of untreated psychological disorders, chronic stress, problematic patterns, and unhealthy habits can mimic drug states. Examining these parallels, along with antecedents that trigger vulnerability toward a particular drug or drug-like state, can help us identify recovery needs underlying the nature of our addictiveness.

Stimulant drugs typically produce a euphoria that is an intense, powerful, narrowly focused energy, without awareness of a clearly defined goal or purpose. Lightness and humor are generally absent and not tolerated from others. A sense of invulnerability and superiority is experienced. Heightened physiological and psychological stress produces anxiety, delusions, disorganized thinking, panic, paranoia, and potential violence.

These euphoric effects are similar to those of a person with untreated bipolar disorder in a manic state. We also see parallels in people with untreated anxiety disorders, perfectionist workaholics, people who seek adrenaline rushes through anger and fighting, or those who chronically create chaotic, crisis-driven lifestyles. Individuals who perpetually overextend themselves, have poor time-management skills, and race from task to task can also fall into this category. And diets of primarily caffeine, sugar, and overly processed food combined with insufficient sleep and relaxation can also produce stimulant-like symptoms.

Usually, there are childhood events that predispose us to create a particular dominant state of mind or being. If our childhood environment included domestic violence, chronic stress, or power struggles, if helplessness, fear, and uncertainty were common, and if excitement was associated with unhealthy behaviors, we may have accepted this model for our own lives. Sometimes, the polar opposite results; life seems boring, constricted, and depressing, and apathy and despair are the dominant emotions. This can also prompt compulsions to experience excitement at any cost, to avoid the internalized deadening feelings. If we choose partners with these tendencies, it is likely that they outwardly express what we feel and deny inwardly.

Opiates simulate a euphoric serenity and pleasurable fulfillment of all of our desires. We are passive, pampered pleasure receivers and there is nothing we need to do. Any mental, emotional, or physical pain or strain is numbed into nonexistence. Thinking is difficult in this floating sensation of peaceful well-being. Apathetic hedonists who exert no personal effort, yet have a means to acquire what they wish from others through inheritance, perceived power or prestige, manipulation, or abuse, and those who have an uncanny knack to attract generous enablers may also experience opiate-like states.

Adults who abuse opiates or who create opiate-like states frequently have an early history of intense conflict between fear and rage, and feel trapped without resources. Varieties of abuse, rejection, and deprivation of basic psychological support, including emotional attunement, are common. Sometimes, however, the childhood experience feels flat and detached, with no one emotionally present or mentally sensitive to verbal or nonverbal cues of danger. The opiate experience for this person, then, is a pleasurable corollary of familiar existence. Choosing a partner with these proclivities often indicates a deep internal passivity and an emotional attachment to a child-like fantasy life, despite the outward reflection of responsibility and task orientation.

Depressant drugs induce a euphoria of positive feelings for self, often to the point of grandiosity. Judgment, perceptions, and inhibitions are depressed, which leaves us free to imagine that our wishes are our reality. Courage, confidence, recklessness, and social ease are typical, as well as a mild dulling of emotional or physical pain. Individuals with narcissistic and borderline personality disorders—often teenagers in groups, and others who demonstrate self-centeredness, entitlement, boisterousness, or overly bold behavior and disregard for or insensitivity toward others—demonstrate depressant-like euphoric symptoms.

Common childhood precursors that make the depressant state attractive are feeling deprived of a sense of personal value and support, deficient social ease, difficulties managing fear, and a sense of abandonment. People who choose partners with this disposition generally have internal conflicts between what they want and what they feel they deserve, and between boundaries and responsibilities.

Recovery includes identifying any unhealthy areas where the drug-like state is produced, and changing the underlying sick beliefs and behaviors. We also need to determine what was present and what was lacking in childhood that triggered addictive vulnerability and then we need to correct for these experiences. We are wise to consciously choose role models who are examples of successful change in areas in which we wish to grow. We should learn all we can about the most mature forms of health in all areas of our lives and incorporate what works for us. In early recovery, we generally start with behavioral and superficial mental and emotional improvements. It is critical to our health and happiness that we continue to develop our capacity for deeper work and deeper change.

....

Personal Growth Questions

1. What feelings do I like to numb and what feelings do I like to magnify? How do I accomplish this?
2. In what ways might my response to childhood be depicted in my attempts toward euphoria?
3. How does my significant other express a part of me that I don't like to show?

Affirmations

I will talk to my support group about
painful feelings and experiences
in order to release them and heal.

I welcome healthy experiences that
stimulate genuine joy, laughter,
serenity, gratitude, and love.

....

Grace Lost and Found

Don't Trust Those Thoughts

If we cease all activity and sit alone and silent for an hour, we will likely discover that our thoughts bear an uncanny resemblance to the utterances of untreated mental patients. If we are addicts or have a history of chronic chaos, depression, stress, trauma, or other dysfunction, there's great likelihood that the most primitive part of our brains have dominant airplay. The lower part of our brain reacts quickly and favors what is familiar, habitual, and likely to bring immediate satisfaction. The more sophisticated part of our brains is slower to reach conclusions because it takes everything into consideration. Not only does it process past and present experiences, and feelings and thoughts on the current topic, it also brainstorms new possibilities and long-range results of all options. Addiction and chronic stress reinforce the lower part and undermine optimal functioning of the higher part of our brains.

So what is the solution to all of this confusion in our minds? We cannot afford to act from old habits, so, until we can identify which thoughts are sick and which are healthy, we refuse to give them power over our decisions or actions. We take direction from those who demonstrate consistently strong recovery principles. We share our experience and listen to others in recovery to learn new tools for thinking and evaluating choices. We identify physical sensations, stirrings of the heart, and intuitive messages as important guides for self-awareness. In addition, we can practice using the higher part of our brains by cultivating patience and tolerance through relaxation and meditation techniques. We begin the process of reconnecting to our hearts through owning our feelings without judgment and establishing a deeper bond with our Higher Power through regular prayer.

Our primitive minds want us to feel pleasure, no matter how brief, and to avoid pain, no matter what the cost, now. Therefore, when we experience overwhelming urgency or anger, grandiosity or self-righteousness, intense need or willfullness, over-controlling tendencies, and/or strong fear of emotional pain, it is likely a sign that our primitive minds are in control. This is when we most need to be reminded of the message of recovery to keep us from sick thinking. It is our responsibility not to endanger or harm ourselves or others, and to thoroughly examine choices and consequences to determine what will help or hamper recovery.

Spiritual principles teach us that our best chance of fulfillment in life is to ask that our Higher Power's will be done through us. Positive thinking and action spurs spiritual growth. Until we are grateful for what we currently have, we will not attract anything better. Until we use the tools that we have, we will not receive more sophisticated ones. Programs advise us not to dwell in negativity, but to identify problems in order to find solutions and grow. For every problem, past or present, there is an internal solution that results in an external demonstration of spiritual strength. Character defects originate to protect us from feeling pain. They end up escalating pain and preventing problem resolution. Character strengths evolve from the courage of surrendering the very defects and defenses that we feel protected us from unalterable pain. The process of healing and growth, therefore, requires a giant leap of faith.

We are here to overcome the difficulties and traumas of our lives. We are here to transform what formerly imprisoned and poisoned us. We are here to surrender defenses and embrace thinking and actions that are proactive in recovery. We are here to bring peace and understanding to the parts inside of us that need healing. We are here to receive wisdom and guidance from the God of our understanding and maintain spiritual fitness as our top priority. We are here to become positive examples to others. We are here to recognize and use our talents to increase goodness in the world. We are here to see that holiness is everywhere when we choose to look deeply. Underneath the worst problem is the most pain. Underneath the pain is an earnest plea for help. It is our task to find the original need and create lives that answer it. Recovery gives us tools to sit alone and silent, and rediscover that we are eternally filled with the love of our God. It is not our thoughts, but our hearts that will lead us here.

Personal Growth Questions

1. What is my biggest fear and how does it control me and my life?
2. What is my greatest talent or gift and how do I use it for myself and others?
3. How can my greatest talent or gift assist me in releasing my greatest fear?

Affirmations

I take time for relaxation exercises or meditation on a daily basis to deepen my conscious contact with my Higher Power.

Through the use of my support group, spiritual principles, and prayer, I find solutions to all of my fears and problems.

....

Perversions of Power

The child's body is braced, rigid with terror. The screams are impotent pleas for protection. The adults ask, how can you be so fragile and frightened? You'll never survive in this world. And they don't stop until they purge all that is innocent out of this child. The child yearns to fly away, but lacks the life force to do so. The child longs to die, but only the heart complies. And then the day arrives for a beautiful escape. Comfort comes from a needle and bliss pours inside. For the first time, insanity is given sweet release. There is no way to know the price of this peace. It feels so safe, secure, and protective. The power of artificial contentment brings new cravings every day, as this child grows into adulthood.

After a while, the adult child takes a companion and becomes a parent. But the poisonous bliss can no longer deaden the rage and pain in these adults. Fear, helplessness, neediness, vulnerability, and longing for love come from the child. The parents who are unable to manage the madness inside themselves, and unable to meet the child's needs, respond to the innocent child as a container for their most toxic emotions. All that they suffered a long time ago is now being prompted and passed to the child. The child's screams cannot elicit caring, compassion, or understanding. Instead, the adults respond with a kind of murderous mission, having no conscious awareness as to why this is occurring. How could they, for they would have to return to their own childhood horror.

Both generations of adults in this all-too-common scenario respond to overwhelming internal pain by shifting to external focus. Without healthy assistance to process feelings, heal, understand, and receive protection for the future, we tend to internalize the attitudes and behaviors of those who harm us. We become self-destructive and externalize through addictions, compulsions, and harm to others. Furthermore, children unconsciously remind their parents of themselves and their own experiences as children. Whatever problems the parents have not personally healed trigger negative, defensive responses toward their children when the children express similar actions, feelings, or thoughts. Even when there are no corresponding issues from children, parents often demonstrate strong, inappropriate reactions to their children when they reach an age in which the parent experienced trauma.

External focus does not allow us to resolve significant problems. We acquire increased tolerance, diminishing returns, and eventual backfiring of overused defense mechanisms, just as we do with drugs. Whatever problems we fail to address and resolve directly and internally worsen. As problems become more severe and frequent, we become increasingly confused and dysfunctional in our lives. Our identities are artificial and superficial, with corresponding low self-esteem and poor relationships. The primary means to nurture and educate children is by example, which includes how we think about, feel toward, and treat ourselves and others. In early childhood, it is impossible for children to internalize and demonstrate attitudes and behaviors that parents demand from them but fail to model personally. When parents examine, heal, and grow from their own wounds in childhood to become healthy role models, their children reap the benefits.

Dominant characteristics of perversions of power are abuse, anger, fear, defensiveness, and offensiveness. Characteristics of healthy empowerment are bonding, integrity, respect, responsibility, mutuality, and understanding. As adults, it is not only our right, but our responsibility to manage our own lives, care for our own well-being and that of our children when they are minors, and continue to learn and evolve behaviorally, emotionally, mentally, and spiritually. When we abuse or relinquish this power or usurp others' power, this creates a discordant relationship with ourselves and others.

Abuse of power suggests that this was modeled earlier in our lives, and that we see relationships as the pairing of dominant and submissive partners. Relinquishing personal power in adulthood reflects a belief that we are in some way deficient or incompetent to manage our own lives, or that acceptance and love comes at the price of passivity and dependence. Usurping others' power suggests that we experienced a lack of fairness and equality in our families, and that competition, jealousy, and readiness for conflict are viewed as a requirement for physical or psychological survival. If we have been subjected to abuse or misuse of power, or have subjected others to the same, we deserve healing and support to create healthy, harmonious, and loving expressions of power in relationships.

....

Personal Growth Questions

1. What kind of power did your caretakers demonstrate with you in childhood and how did it feel?
2. As an adult, what kind of power do you manifest and how does it feel?
3. What internal changes can you make to express healthier and more loving power in your current life?

Affirmations

I am capable of resolving past harm and
releasing the negative energy from inside of me.

I choose to experience healthy empowerment
and harmonious reciprocal relationships.

....

Transformations

How does inferiority become humility? How does narcissism become healthy self-love? How does arrogance become confidence? How does superiority become positive self-esteem?

By removing fear. Fear arises from internalizing mistreatment and deprivation. We personalize problems without solutions when we have no other tools. We take on others' problems when we lack a sense of wholeness. We compare, compete, and judge when we view life as limited.

When we're cynical and pessimistic, we've internalized helplessness. When we're apathetic, bored, and numb, we're afraid of being overwhelmed. Obsessions and compulsions represent fear of self-examination and change. Recklessness and abuse arise from fears that our lives don't matter. If we whine, complain, plead, lie, manipulate, intimidate, or threaten to get our needs met, we have the wrong needs. And we lost our real selves a long time ago.

Pain experienced without healthy tools to process and understand it can pull us away from our real selves, as well as from others and from life itself. Whether we withdraw passively or aggressively, the latter through hostile behaviors and attitudes, we depart from a spiritual sense of life. The further we are from our spiritual source, the more fear we experience and the more we settle for empty substitutes of who we truly are and what our lives can be.

Our real selves are who we are when we are honest about our struggles, defenses, and wounds, as well as about our talents, gifts, and accomplishments. We are real and whole when we respond to pain and problems by remaining close to ourselves and others who can help us learn and grow. Conflicts and crises then allow us to re-examine and understand ourselves with greater depth and compassion. In this way, we realize new strengths from struggles.

If we live focusing on what we need and don't have, we live in fear. If we live focusing on gratitude for what we have and let our desires lead us to work on personal change to attract those things, we live in love. If we live believing that when we attain some external goal we'll gain an internal quality, we live in fear. (For example, "When I'm rich, I'll be generous to others." or "When I have a girlfriend, I'll be happy.") By contrast, if we live with awareness of internal riches, our outward lives flourish.

When our attachment lies in seeking, we find more to seek. Then when a desire happens to be fulfilled, instead of feeling grateful and happy, we identify more desires. When this is our pattern of thinking, we can receive love from the person from whom we most desire love, and it will not diminish our seeking. We will find fault with the amount, the motivation, potential longevity, or the way love was given. This pattern arises when past internalized feelings of deprivation and incompleteness block or sabotage current satisfaction and fulfillment—when we have over-identified ourselves so strongly with deprivation that we impose it on even the most fulfilling of circumstances.

We must, therefore, change our thinking about our identities and our lives so that we create and reinforce conditions receptive to fulfillment. Paying attention to what we love and admire, and discovering where it exists inside of us, recalls our true selves to conscious awareness. When we cannot see what we admire and love in ourselves, we need to identify and remove whatever blocks this. Appreciation, gratitude, joy, love, and serenity start with us. Inability to see our character strengths means that we have built a defensive wall around them in response to an earlier environment that did not support them. Removing these walls that came from fear, deprivation, and harm allows us to see our true selves, our purpose, and the deeper meaning of life. This is how we embrace our primary identities as spiritual beings.

When we remember that we are connected to a healthy Higher Power, we know that we have an unlimited supply of love, wisdom, and understanding. If we identify the character strengths that we associate with living our ideal lives, and practice demonstrating these qualities to help ourselves and others, we will attract our ideals. What we truly value and hold most dear to us reflects our highest selves. Allowing our highest selves to guide us into positive action is a magnet for fulfillment. When our daily lives evolve from this awareness, character defects are transformed into positive qualities.

....

Personal Growth Questions

1. What is one area of my life that I wish to positively transform and why?
2. What character strengths do I need to demonstrate in order to achieve this transformation?
3. What fears must I release in order to transform?

Affirmations

*I am created from divine love
and I have the ability to transform all
challenges into spiritual growth.*

*I willingly release all that
blocks me from my highest potential.*

....

Epilogue

I WISH TO LEAVE YOU, at the end of this book, with some new thoughts about an old children's nursery rhyme. The song "Row, Row, Row Your Boat" offers spiritual guidance when we view it metaphorically. I will give you my ideas of the enlightened and the unenlightened meaning of this simple song.

"Row, row, row your boat" suggests that we are responsible for our life and for learning to use the tools we've been given to do our part well. We often counter this by waiting for something or someone to row or push our boat, and then assign blame because we're going the wrong way. Or we may tell others how to row their boats. Or perhaps we'll get in and row their boats for them, neglecting our own. Finally, we may just sit in our boat, hoping that no one tries to overturn it. We wonder why life is bewildering.

"Gently down the stream" advises us to surrender defenses, defects, negative energies, and "fixes," and let the God of our understanding guide us in divine flow. Often, we worry that we're not going far enough, fast enough, or not reaching our goal. We may complain that other people sabotage our progress. Then, when we arrive at our harbor, we notice only what's wrong with the place, and conclude that life is a difficult, uphill battle.

"Merrily, merrily, merrily, merrily" indicates that happiness is created within us. It is the deepest, most natural part of our true self. We may believe, however, that our happiness depends on reaching certain goals. And when we fail to find happiness upon those achievements, we quickly set new ambitions. Now life is a treadmill.

"Life is but a dream" tells us that our higher self is spiritual, our higher home is heavenly, and our purpose is to awaken to eternal truth. Conversely, we may think that life is a rat race, and the one who dies with the most toys wins. Or we may view life as frightening, meaningless, or punitive.

I will continue with the boat analogy to illustrate how it applies to some common compulsions. In substance abuse, we've lost our oars and our boat is full of holes, but we imagine ourselves in yachts. In codependence, we're in somebody else's boat playing tug-of-war with their oars. With eating disorders, we're holding our oars tightly to our body, so that no one else can take them. When we're workaholics, we think we're in a race, so we row as fast as we can. In compulsive gambling, we're pirates, envying and trying to capture other people's boats. In sex addiction, we lust for others' oars, or row in circles with our own oars.

We typically live the unenlightened version of rowing our boats initially, then hit bottom in some way, and ultimately ideally transform. We can't become great sea captains on tranquil waters. We don't evolve in our ability to love, when only loving people surround us. Those who anger and upset us indicate the areas within us that need and deserve healing. We can surrender addictions and compulsions, but until we elevate our spiritual consciousness, satisfaction and serenity elude us. Healing must transform our entire view of ourselves and life. This, then, gives us the powerful treasures of humility, gratitude, and generosity. Life is now filled with grace. When willfulness becomes willingness, deceit becomes honesty, and rigid habits become open-mindedness, we can receive what Heaven wants to give us: the memory that we are divinely created miracles surrounded by divinely created miracles.

About the Author

MARY COOK HOLDS A MASTER'S DEGREE in psychology and is a registered addiction specialist, with thirty-four years of clinical experience and twenty-nine years of university teaching experience. She has a private practice providing telephone and office counseling, as well as in-service training seminars, workshops, and guided meditation. Mary is a national speaker and has been a contributing editor for "Steps for Recovery" since 2001. Find her at *www.marycookMA.com*

To Our Readers

CONARI PRESS, an imprint of Red Wheel/Weiser, publishes books on topics ranging from spirituality, personal growth, and relationships to women's issues, parenting, and social issues. Our mission is to publish quality books that will make a difference in people's lives—how we feel about ourselves and how we relate to one another. We value integrity, compassion, and receptivity, both in the books we publish and in the way we do business.

Our readers are our most important resources, and we value your input, suggestions, and ideas about what you would like to see published. Please feel free to contact us, to request our latest book catalog, or to be added to our mailing list.

Conari Press
An imprint of Red Wheel/Weiser, LLC
500 Third Street, Suite 230
San Francisco, CA 94107
www.redwheelweiser.com